THE ART OF EFFECTIVE
MENTORING

DAON MCLARIN JOHNSON

The Art of Effective Mentoring

Imagination Press, LLC

First Edition: June 2021

Editing by
Doc Wilson
Teresa Hamilton
Brandi Dyer
Tyler LaRoche

Cover Artwork - "The Angel of Chastains Row" by David W. M. Cassidy

Layout by
Francis Adams

ISBN: 978-1-7337189-9-8

School's Out – The Artwork of Allan Crite: Museum of Modern Art

The Art of Effective Mentoring
Similar to faint brushes on a blank canvas...
or soft notes melodiously whispered in the midst of a concerto,
effective mentoring requires both theory and practice,
structure and improvisation
chorus and cadenza
forte and diminuendo
to produce a harmonious blend
of personal and professional success
in the life of a protégé.

Yes! Mentoring is an art!

Daon McLarin Johnson

APPRECIATION

Dr. Anita Lyons
Cheryl Sidwell
Sterling Owens
Dr. Shekeitha Jeffries
Evangela Wimbush
Cousin Teresa Hamilton

DEDICATIONS

The characters in *The Art of Effective Mentoring* are shoutouts to a few of the many individuals that have walked with me in the journey of mentoring the next generation of leaders. They are listed in order of appearance...

Danielle Milner-Middlebrooks as Alexandra Milner-Middlebrooks
Lisa Nicole Briellen Johnson as Rena Briellen
Danise DiStasi as Danise DiStasi
Freddie Allen Nolen as Freddie Nolen
Richard Shawn Warner as Shawn Richard
Sheila Sathe-Warner as Sheila Rowan
Kevin Robbs as Troy Robbs
Troy D. Lewis, II as Troy Robbs
Joshua Cruse as Anderson Cruse
Joseph S. Somerville, III as Joe Somers
Isaiah T. Farmer as Isaiah Minor
Kashieka Minor as Ms. Minor
Kevin Brown as Kevin Brown
Junior Sidwell – Writing Companion/Golden Retriever
Cherl Sidwell, Co-Author as Cheryl Saylor
Onnie Kirk, "Enjoy the Journey"
Dakari Taylor-Watson as Mr. Dakari
Raymond Reeves as Raymond Reevson
Fred McCray as Fred McCrayson
William Calvin Henderson
Quntavius Devei Johnson
The Mentors of Mentoring to Manhood
The Moms of Mentoring to Manhood

THE ARTISTS

Rudi Nofiandri – "My name is Rudi Nofiandri, but my friends call me Rudi. I currently live in Koto Padang, Sumatera Barat, Indonesia, I am 31 years old. I am the second of four siblings. I graduated with a bachelor's degree in social and political science from Universitas Andalas. I started my career as a graphic designer in 2011.

From a young age, I had hobbies and talents in arts such as painting and music. I studied graphic design by myself. It all started when I often saw friends making design work, and I started learning it through YouTube.

Graphic design is very important to me because it can train my creativity and I am very happy to do it because I can work with a hobby. With this graphic design I can make my parents and my wife happy."

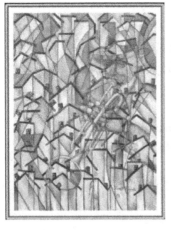

David W. M Cassidy - David W. M. Cassidy grew up in Compton and Los Angeles California. Graduated from George Washington (now Preparatory) High School in 1973. He received a B. A. in Urban and Rural Studies, University of California, San Diego, Third College, 1978. He served in the United States Navy as a Hospital man (Hm2), Field Medical Tech, X-Ray Tech, and Emergency Medical Tech. A graduate of the Interdenominational Theological Center (ITC), C.H. Mason Seminary, 1990 graduated with honors and received the Master of Divinity degree.

Rev. Dave was licensed in 1982, and ordained in 1990 by Bishop George Dallas McKinney Jr., Southern California 2nd Ecclesiastical Jurisdiction, of the Church of God in Christ.

David W. Cassidy is a published writer, a published artist. He is a self-taught artist who has had no formal artistic education post high school. His medium of choice is oil painting. He is known for a cubist abstractionist style, the boldness of expression and attention to details of color and composition in his paintings. His artwork is owned by over 60 collectors through the United States and Africa. Author of, The Art of My Life, Blurb.com, and he has designed artwork for United Methodist Publishing House VBS projects; African Methodist Episcopal Church Devotionals, book covers, etc.

David W. Cassidy lives in Upper Marlboro, MD and is married to Rev. Lillian Catherine Smith, Pastor of Cheverly United Methodist Church, Cheverly, MD. He and Lillian have two sons, David Charles Jasper Smith-Cassidy and Hayward Felton Earl Smith-Cassidy.

Hey there! My name is **Brandon Herbert**. I am a graphic designer, entrepreneur, former mentee, and student, but I'm always learning. My vision is to create designs that influence what we think, the way we feel, and the decisions we make. I learned a lot from being around many mentors and fellow mentees during my time at Mentoring to Manhood. I gained a lot of skills as well as strong morals that I'll be taking with me into manhood. Hopefully, you get a taste of those learning moments while reading this book.

A little background about me. I was born in Washington, DC, raised for a couple of years in Baltimore, and relocated for middle school, high school, and college, to Bowie, Maryland. Currently, l reside in Bowie, Maryland with my family. While I am no longer chasing my degree in digital media - my area of expertise, I own a Graphic Design Business. With it, I've achieved a lot of goals for myself, but my biggest achievement to date is that I paid off my student loans the first day I could. A lot of students who even go for all four years have to worry about paying off debts, interest on payments, fees, and more. The responsibility and accountability required of me after making the decision to leave were all with the help of the many mentors, or teachers around me.

My future goals include expanding my graphic design company, BBD, or BrazyBran Design Studios to better facilitate the rollout of new services. As the days go by, I spend time acquiring new skills to offer. My plan is to become a leader in the 3D art and design, video production, filmmaking, and video game development. In addition, I may even venture into BBD apparel for individuals of all sizes and shapes. In short, what I've built for my business, to this day, is a strong base that allows me to go into any room I choose with confidence in the services that I provide. **For what the future holds ... there is no ceiling!**

Joseph Ferguson – Joseph Ferguson, Jr. is currently a junior at the Duke Ellington School of the Arts in Washington, DC. Affectionately known as, "Pino", by his mom. (But please don't tell anybody) At the tender age of 5 months, the "unique firecracker" already began to show signs of greatness. A very inquisitive child, Joseph taught himself various skills, such as, knitting, sewing, 3D printing, designing shirts and sketching. Currently, Joseph is an inspired artist and what is so unique and astounding, he is completely self-taught! Joseph has recently expressed an interest in media and communication. Not sure what career path he will choose, but we do know acceleration will be the outcome! Lovingly submitted by Mom, LaBreshia Butler

WORDS FROM THE CO-AUTHOR

One year ago, in March 2020, I was working for Wicomico Public Libraries when the world abruptly came to a halt. COVID-19 made its way into Maryland, and everything shut down. Suddenly, I was working from home, navigating a new "virtual world" and adding words like "Zoom" to my vocabulary.

One day, as I was scrolling through social media, I saw a post on my Facebook page from my long-time friend, Daon. It caught my eye because Daon is never on Facebook. He asked if I had a picture of our Kindergarten class. I thought it was a strange request, but I looked around and could not find one. I emailed him my reply, and he told me the real reason he was contacting me – he was writing his second book on the "The Art of Mentoring", and would I be interested in collaborating?

My first thought was, why me? I thought it was strange and synchronistic that my friend was asking me to be part of a project on mentoring, because I had recently been thinking a great deal about this very subject – about how to mentor young people, and give back to my community. I was particularly interested in mentoring young women because I never really experienced that growing up. I was blessed with supportive parents and some incredible teachers (many of whom Daon and I shared), but no one who really "mentored" me on my direction in life – who helped me reveal and develop my strengths and with "unconditional positive regard", supported my dreams for the future. As a consequence, even though I was a good student, who achieved high marks in school, I often felt like I was floundering – especially in college, where I literally had no guidance on choosing a career path, or figuring out what I needed to do to get where I wanted to go.

Much later in life, I was fortunate to experience mentorship on my spiritual path through the teachings and guidance of Sam "Caocoochee" Thomas and other spiritual teachers. The impact these teachers had on helping me to become who I am today cannot be measured – they mentored the most important part of me – and helped me to become the teacher I am today.

I was intrigued by the idea of working on this project, and honored that Daon asked me to collaborate, as I have the utmost respect for him and his work mentoring youth. During the past year when "social distancing" became the "norm", Daon and I continued to meet over weekly Zoom calls to work on "The Art of Effective Mentoring". I enjoyed reconnecting with my old friend, and helping to develop the character's stories. Somehow, it made this very strange time in history a little bit easier. At some point, even my golden retriever, Junior, made an appearance in the book. As the stories developed, I also began to realize how much I have learned on my own journey in pursuit of living a meaningful life.

It's been a long time since the days we learned the letters of the alphabet in Mrs. Henson's Kindergarten class. So much has happened in the world since those innocent days of laughter, growth and friendship, but collaborating on this book reminds me of the promising future I envisioned back then, and gives me hope for the next generation of leaders. My deepest gratitude to Daon for inviting me to be part of this experience, and to all of my teachers who acted as mentors on the journey of life.

- Cheryl Sidwell

PREFACE

The lightbulb just went off for me. Sitting here at my desk in the basement of my home, I had an otherworldly epiphany! I just realized that I probably learned the art of effective mentoring from Helen McLarin Johnson[1].

"Who is Helen McLarin Johnson?" you might ask!

Well, Helen Johnson was and is my mother. She was a second grade public school teacher who instilled in me the importance of mentoring. For over thirty years, Mrs. Johnson, as she was affectionately called by students, parents, community leaders and church-goers, drove to her elementary school in Arnold, Maryland and dedicated her life to mentoring future leaders. She labored in a meticulously and strategically designed classroom that empowered and equipped all sorts of learners (fast, slow, tactile, aural, visual, verbal, and all variations in between) to utilize their inherent gifts and talents to achieve greatness.

Without all the fanfare, accolades or a shining spotlight, Helen McLarin Johnson used her platform as a teacher to educate literally thousands of human beings about the fundamental principles of reading, writing and arithmetic. However, in addition to the pedagogy of the rudimentary basics, Helen McLarin Johnson also instilled within the hearts of her protégés a love for learning, growing, and strengthening their capacity to assimilate knowledge. I believe this love for learning and betterment is the pinnacle of educational and artistic achievement, but I also believe that it is the distinction that separates an ordinary teacher from a teacher that is a mentor.

Incessantly reading and expanding her expertise, Helen McLarin Johnson was the absolute personification of the terms 'professional development' and 'continuing education.' And although second graders are not particularly concerned with learning styles or pedagogical theory, they are inherently attuned to a teacher who genuinely cares. And that is exactly what effective mentors do - they genuinely care. Make no mistake, **genuine concern is one of the central elements of the powerful art of mentoring**. It is the delineation between transactional instruction and transformational impartation.

Suzanne Faure, an expert in the field of mentorship, defines mentoring thusly, "Mentoring is a supportive learning relationship between a caring individual who shares knowledge, experience and wisdom with another individual who is ready and willing to benefit from this exchange, to enrich their professional journey[2]."

This book will outline several definitions for The Art of Effective Mentoring. These definitions will intersect and move fluidly throughout the book as we examine varying modes and methods to The Art of Effective Mentoring; but at this juncture, I will propose our first definition:

> *"Mentoring is the timeless discipline that interconnects individuals for the purpose of sharing collective experiences, and exchanging personal and professional knowledge that results in transformation that lasts a lifetime."*
> - Daon McLarin Johnson

Yes, I realize that this first definition is a little heady and theoretical, but it will suffice as an introductory remark. For the purpose of this book, I believe we should also take the mentoring definition one step further: mentoring is significantly more than a mere classification, theoretical framework, or ethereal abstract. Effective mentoring is more fluid, more creative, and more imaginative. Mentoring is akin to a symphonic interaction between two individuals for the purpose of creating a personal and professional masterpiece in the life of the mentee. Similar to faint brushes on a blank

[2]Andrew Gibbons. https://www.trainingjournal.com/blog/16-mentoringdefinitions

canvas, or soft notes melodiously whispered in the midst of a concerto, **effective mentoring requires both theory and practice, structure and improvisation chorus, and cadenza forte and diminuendo to produce a harmonious blend of personal and professional success in the life of a protégé.** Yes! Mentoring is an art!

The Art of Effective Mentoring has been divided into three sections – just like a symphony with three movements.

Movement One – Preparing the Canvas will focus on the elemental groundwork that must be undertaken at the beginning of every effective mentor-mentee relationship. Sculptors call this stage, **"Carving"** – which seeks to provide the reader, the mentor, and/or the mentoring organization with a powerful foundation on which to build a mentoring relationship and a mentoring program. This foundation is rooted in the establishment of clear expectations and parameters of the mentoring engagement.

Movement Two – Painting the Canvas will serve as the central focus of the book, and includes the essential methodology, techniques, and skills that are essential to mentor the next generation of leaders. Artists who sculpt call this stage **"Modeling"** – in which we will delineate best practices and provide practical, grass-roots tips for developing and maintaining a successful mentoring relationship. Leading by example, and listening between the lines, are a few of the skills paramount to effective mentoring.

Movement Three – The Finishing Touches will discuss the important concept of closure that must be considered at the conclusion of each mentoring engagement. Sculptors call this final phase **"Assembly"** – in which we will highlight the necessary assessments that must take place to launch the mentor and protégé into a successful personal and professional space after the formal mentoring relationship concludes.

Recently, I informally asked a group of successful men and women about their primary motivation for serving as mentors. Simon Sinek refers to it as **"What's your why?"** Although the responses were varied and quite multifaceted, I came to the non-empirical conclusion that there are **two**

primary motivations for the individual who answers the call to mentor the next generation of leaders: **"giving back"** and **"the aha moment."**

The Motivation to Give Back

The first motivation is the internal drive to "give back"; some would call this "paying it forward." Others would correlate this motivation to the desire to **make an eternal contribution to humanity, or to leave a legacy that will last far beyond their finite and ephemeral, seventy-plus year human lifespan.** This motivation very well might be the main reason that you are reading this manual. You have a strong desire to contribute to the next generation because, at one time in your life, someone took the time and initiative to give to you. You are grateful and, consequently, you are motivated by a strong spirit of reciprocity.

The Motivation of the "Aha Moment"

The second motivation that seems to equally drive mentors to interact with their protégé is what we term the "aha moment." The "aha moment" occurs when a protégé (young or old, personal or professional) encounters and assimilates revelatory information for the very first time. John Koniounous and Mark Beeman define this phenomenon as the **"Cognitive Neuroscience of Insight."** This powerfully pointed phenomenon occurs universally throughout the human race – regardless of genetic makeup, culture, or environment. It manifests universally when a homo-sapiens (for the purpose of our manual - a mentee) suddenly comprehends a concept or event that solves a problem, reinterprets a situation, explains a joke, or resolves an ambiguous precept.

In practice, the mentors have stated that **"there is nothing like the feeling that occurs when the light goes on in my mentee's eyes."** Consequently, whenever a revelation or connection is made, when a leap of faith is made, a milestone is reached, a sought-after accomplishment is achieved, or a hard-fought goal is attained, the protégé's eyes light up, and an overwhelming sense of gratitude occurs in the heart of the mentee. This phenomenon, experienced by the mentee, and witnessed by the mentor, is an incredibly powerful motivator!

Oddly enough, that is what I am experiencing as we set out to discuss The Art of Effective Mentoring. Yes, indeed, I am experiencing the cognitive neuroscience of insight. Aha! I earlier referred to this as an 'epiphany.' I have realized, much to my surprise, that Helen McLarin Johnson is still mentoring me even at this moment. Her words, **"Daon, you can do anything you set your little heart to do!" continue to reverberate in my psyche whenever I encounter an obstacle.** But not only Helen McLarin Johnson, but I also acknowledge many other men and women who have transformed me and made indelible footprints on the canvas of my heart and soul. And what has ensued, is a powerful sense of gratitude for my many mentors who have embraced The Art of Effective Mentoring, and taught me to do the same.

Leave a Legacy,
Daon McLarin Johnson

TABLE OF CONTENTS

TABLE OF CONTENTS

\

INTRODUCTION

"The greatest good you can do for another is not just to share your riches, but to reveal to him his own."

- Benjamin Disraeli

"He's like my big brother, I truly hate having discussions about who would win one-on-one, or fans saying, 'Hey, Kobe', you'd beat Michael one-on-one.' I feel like, what you get from me is from him. I don't get five championships here without him because he guided me so much and gave me so much great advice." Kobe Bryant What is a mentor? Is there a difference between a mentor and a counselor? Is there a distinction between a mentor and an advisor? What distinguishes a mentor from a coach, a teacher, or a therapist?

A few years had gone by since her husband had passed. As a matter of fact, this night was the anniversary of his untimely death. It should also be noted that tonight was the first time that, Mildred Cox, had gathered the nerves to see her famous grandson play. Up until then, watching her grandson play in youth leagues and high school was "too nerve wracking."

Up until now, the anxiety and stress from watching her grandson play in an arena of twenty thousand critics was more than she could ever bear. But tonight, was different. Tonight, would be the first time that Mrs. Cox had seen her grandson play live and in person. It should also be noted that this first time viewing was taking place at the iconic Staple Center in Inglewood, California.

After a rather uneventful first half, it was already the third quarter, and the Los Angeles Lakers were trailing the Toronto Raptors by eighteen points. Phil Jackson, the quintessential basketball guru stood motionless on the side as he always did. Then it happened. Mildred Cox's grandson scored two points, then another two points, then a three-pointer, then another three-pointer. By the end of the third quarter, Mildred's grandson had scored an eye-opening twenty-seven points. But that wasn't all. At the end of the fourth quarter, her young grandson, who had caused her so much stress and anxiety, had drained another twenty-eight points. When all was said and done, her grandson, Kobe Bryant, had made seven three-pointers, and sunk 18-of-20 from the foul line, for a mind-boggling total of 81 points – second in NBA history only to Wilt Chamberlain.

Kobe Bryant would later attribute his historic performance to the fact that his grandmother had attended her first and only NBA game on that enchanting evening. But then, I began to wonder: who mentored Kobe Bryant? Who did my absolute favorite player of all time look to when he needed advice or simply a listening ear? Who was Kobe Bryant's mentor? This question intrigued me. Reader, please allow me a second to explain.

You Know It (Effective Mentoring) When You See It
Every mentoring book that I have read, invariably starts out with a section or entire chapter devoted to demarking what distinguishes mentoring from all other instructional and psychological disciplines. Here are few of these definitions...

- Advisor - a person who gives advice in a particular field
- Coach - an athletic instructor or trainer
- Counselor - a person trained to give guidance on personal, social or psychological problems
- Guru - an influential teacher or popular expert
- Motivator - a person who promotes interest in, or enthusiasm for, something
- Teacher - a person who teaches – especially in a school

From these definitions, I hope you would agree that coaching and teaching are transactional disciplines that propagate the development of skill and the acquisition of knowledge. In other words, coaching and teaching are transactions between a producer and a consumer. In both instances, the student is provided with information with the explicit intention to learn or improve competencies and capabilities. Similarly, advisors, counselors and therapists are also transactional disciplines that seek to impart specific circumstantial solutions to particular incidences and isolated challenges.

My premise, however, is that, even though a mentor invariably functions in all of these transactional disciplines, not all of these professionals can simultaneously be referred to as "mentors." For example, all of us have experienced a teacher who dryly espoused principles and formulas (while we gazed out the window), or a coach who taught the difference between a zone defense versus man-to-man. Yet, we look back and can hardly remember their names because their interactions had no transforming affect – merely transactions. So, what's the demarcation? **The Art of Effective Mentoring** will answer that burning question.

When someone like Oprah Winfrey opens her mouth and utters the words referring to Maya Angelou, "I had many advisors, but she was like a MENTOR to me," or when Jody Adams-Birch says of Pat Summit, "I had many coaches, but she was my MENTOR," we all understand that being a MENTOR is infinitely more than an advisor, a teacher, or a coach. **Being a MENTOR means that the individual possesses** a secret sauce that other advisors, coaches, teachers, and supervisors do not possess. Being a MENTOR inexplicably carries a greater weight, a greater gravitas that is difficult to identify or explain. We can't necessarily put our finger on it, but we know that it is something special, a secret sauce, and "we know it when we see it."

In these instances, the interactions between the two individuals are more than transactional exchanges. **The connections are significantly deeper, and carry emotional weight.** I would assert that the interactions between Oprah Winfrey and Maya Angelou, and Jody Adams-Birch and Pat Summit, were not just transactional; rather, they were transformational. As I stated in the foreword, they convey genuine care. Maya Angelou and Pat Summit possessed that "secret sauce." Their interactions were far beyond the intellectual impartation of facts, knowledge or diagrams on a white-board;

their interactions left indelible footprints on the heart of the mentee that proved to be eternally transformational. This is "The Art of Effective Mentoring."

Isn't this true of the mentors in your life? Stephen E Kohn and Vincent D. O'Connell have written, "Mentoring creates an emotional connection that is rather unique to teaching, guidance, and professional support processes. We have found that the true nature of mentoring is embedded within the following statement a mentee might make: **"S/he is more than a teacher / manager/ supervisor / counselor to me - s/he is my MENTOR."[3]** This is "The Art of Effective Mentoring."

This brings us full circle to Kobe Bryant. I am sure that he had many teachers, coaches, advisors, and motivators in his life. But who did the Black Mamba personally elevate to the status of mentor? What characteristics did they possess? Who mentors greatness? The answer lies in the following: If one seeks to be powerful, he must be mentored by one with power. If one seeks to be skillful, he must be mentored by one with great skill. **If one seeks to leave a legacy, he must be mentored by one who has left a legacy.** This, too, is "The Art of Effective Mentoring."

It should then come as no surprise that Michael Jordan was one of Kobe Bryant's mentors. While watching the Last Dance, it became obvious that there was a unique relationship between Michael Jordan (mentor) and Kobe Bryant (protégé). Morpheus and Neo come to mind, or maybe Daniel LaRusso and Mr. Miyagi. Beyond the late-night calls, the postgame debriefs and the hours of watching film, Jordan and Bryant's interactions proved to be one of the foundational elements of Bryant's greatness. **Greatness mentors greatness.** And the interactions, conversations and impartations are not transactional; rather, they are powerfully transformational. The result, eighty-one points and a performance that will be remembered forever. It should therefore come as no surprise that the profound effect that Michael had on Kobe is the exact same profound effect that Kobe had on us all. This is *The Art of Effective Mentoring*.

[3]Kohn & O'Connell. 9 Powerful Practices of Really Great Mentors

The Art of Effective Mentoring

"Mentoring is the timeless discipline that interconnects individuals for the purpose of sharing collective experiences while exchanging and increasing personal and professional knowledge resulting in transformation that lasts a lifetime."
- Daon McLarin Johnson

SECTION

PREPARING THE CANVAS

PREPARING THE CANVAS

Preparing the Canvas, consisting of the first three chapters, will focus on the elemental groundwork required at the beginning of every effective mentor-mentee relationship. Sculptors call this stage "Carving."

This section seeks to provide the reader, the mentor, and/or the mentoring organization, with a powerful foundation on which to build the mentoring relationship, and a mentoring program. The Art of Mentoring will divide this first movement of our symphony into three stages:

- LEGISLATING
- LEAVING
- LABORING

Chapter One, LEGISLATING, puts forth the important element of the mentoring agreement, and how it plays a critical role in establishing and sustaining the structure and stability of the mentoring relationship.

Chapter Two, LEAVING, promotes the importance of explicitly discussing how the mentoring relationship will end. It is essential that the discussion of closure takes place at the outset of the mentoring relationship to circumvent potential frustration and unmet expectations.

Chapter Three, LABORING, details the important groundwork of setting goals, and charting a path for character growth and development. Discussions on these topics should take place at the beginning of the mentoring relationship. In addition, these discussions must actively include the thoughts and input of the mentee to ensure the relationship's success.

Let the artwork begin!

CHAPTER ONE

LEGISLATION

Every formal mentoring relationship should begin
with clear expectations for both the mentor and mentee.

"My mentor said, 'Let's go do it,' not 'You go do it.'
How powerful when someone says, 'Let's!'"
- Jim Rohn

"Mentoring is a brain to pick, an ear to listen
and a push in the right direction."
- John Crosby

"Millennials don't want to be managed, they like to be led, coached, and
mentored. This generation is on fire and ready to go.
Are you ready to change the world?"
- Farshad Asl

Meet Alexandra, the Mentor and Rena, the Mentee

Opening Day

Four years of undergraduate education, a 4.13 grade point average, multiple honor society inductions, student government, a semester abroad, and two internships had not completely prepared Rena for this moment – the first day on her first "real" job. Even though her external appearance conveyed poise and absolute confidence as she strode into the glass encased high-rise office building, the uncertainty of her immediate future had taken a terrible toll on her mental well-being.

At the same time that Rena opened the heavy glass door to enter the south end of the lobby, a loud chime signaled the arrival of the elevator. The large stainless steel doors slid open, and Alexandra Milner Middlebrooks, the head of the finance department, emerged with an inexplicably calm demeanor. She took a few steps forward, and instantly recognized their company's new hire, Rena Briellen.

"Hello Rena! How are you today?" Alexandra's radiant smile and warm welcome filled the lobby. "My name is Alexandra. I will be serving as your corporate mentor during the first year of your employment with Strategion Enterprises."

Rena smiled, momentarily overriding the great sense of anxiety that had lodged like an ulcer in the pit of her stomach. "Hello, Alexandra. I am very

4

pleased to meet you. Thank you for your warm welcome." Rena secretly wondered if Alexandra could sense the immediate relief that she had felt upon hearing Alexandra's first words.

Oddly enough, when Alexandra had first agreed to Strategion's new mentoring initiative, she had not been highly receptive to the idea. In fact, no one in her department was. To Alexandra's initial chagrin, after several meetings with consultants and mentoring experts, Strategion's human resources department had unanimously decided to move forward with a mentoring program for its new executives and managers. The mentoring program would be supervised by Strategion's newly hired Dean of Leadership Development, Danise DiStasi.

The statistics were overwhelmingly in the mentorship program's favor.

For CEOs' in a formal mentoring program,

- 84% of CEO's said that mentors had helped them avoid costly mistakes
- 84% of CEO's said that they became proficient in their role faster
- 69% were making better decisions[4]

- Research also showed:

- Mentees are promoted five times more often than those not in a mentoring program
- Retention rates are higher for both mentees (22% more) and mentors (20% more) than for employees who did not participate in a mentoring program[5]
- Millennials who intended to stay with their organization for more than five years, are twice as likely to have a mentor (68%) than not (32%)
- Participants are 40% more likely to achieve their goals if they write them down. This increases to 70% if the goals are shared with someone to keep them accountable, such as a mentor.

[4]Harvard Business Review 2015. https://mccarthymentoring.com/whymentoring-what-the-stats-say/
[5] Gartner 2006. https://mccarthymentoring.com/why-mentoring-what-thestats-say/

- 89% of those mentored, go on to mentor others – thus contributing to a culture of learning and mentoring

Three months ago, when Strategion pushed forward and released the company-wide memo rolling out their corporate mentoring program, Alexandra responded affirmatively, but with a hint of annoyance and ambivalence. "How was she, or any of her colleagues, going to be able to squeeze a mentoring project into an already exhausting sixty-hour work week?"

In spite of her outward affirmative response, there remained uneasy feelings, as well as a smattering of skepticism that Alexandra simply could not disregard – actually, the same questions that plagued most new mentors:

- What was she getting into?
- How much of her time would be required?
- Was this a long-term commitment?
- How often would she have to communicate with her mentee?
- What if her mentee was a putz?
- How would she measure her success as a mentor?

Fortunately, as Alexandra stepped out of the elevator, the majority and most pressing of her concerns were minimized because they had been addressed by a comprehensive mentor training program recently instituted by Strategion. The training program, also led by Danise DiStasi, successfully eased Alexandra's fears (and the fears of her colleagues) because Strategion had provided its managers with the tools and tricks-of-the-trade to be effective mentors for each of their prospective mentees.

But it had not always been so. Two years previously, Strategion had attempted to launch a mentoring initiative that failed miserably because of the company's inability to clearly delineate expectations and requirements for the participants in its program - both for mentors and mentees. The short-lived program never gained traction because mentors and mentees alike expressed frustration with unmet expectations, vague program parameters, and lack of adequate mentoring methodology.

Getting Acquainted

Alexandra started walking. Her long strides reflected her confidence. "Rena, let me show you to your office. I know that you have several meetings on your agenda for today. The first meeting is at 9:30 am, and will be with your immediate supervisor. I believe you met him during your second round of interviews."

Rena nodded, attempting to match strides with her new mentor.

"Freddie is definitely one of the bright stars in our marketing department. After Freddie, you will have a brief break, during which Danise, from HR, will give you a more formal tour of the facility, and provide you with the details of our onboarding process. Finally, you will have an opportunity to participate in your first bi-weekly marketing strategy meeting. Freddie will be there, but this will also allow you to meet the other members of your marketing team. Finally, at the end of your day, you and I will circle back to go over the terms and expectations of our mentoring contract and answer any questions that you might have."

Rena continued to take it all in. She felt like she was drinking water from a firehose, but she definitely appreciated having Alexandra in her corner.

"Here is your new office; decorate it as you wish. Office supplies are in the closet at the end of the hall." Alexandra took a deep breath and paused, "I know that this was a lot to take in on your first day. On my first day, I was an absolute nervous wreck! Though cool on the outside, my insides were churning.

How are YOU feeling?" asked Alexandra.

Rena smiled, "I'm feeling pretty good. A little nervous, but pretty good. Thank you for taking time out of your busy schedule to show me around."

Alexandra, continuing to make eye contact, asked, "Do I have your permission to ask you one important question before you get started on your day?"

Rena nodded in the affirmative, "Sure, what is it?"

Alexandra smiled, "Can you share with me one positive thing that has happened to you recently? It can be personal or professional[6]."

Rena had to think for a moment. The question caught her off guard and required her to shift her thinking and mindset. In a split second, she knew what to do. She smiled and said, "One positive thing is the fact that my transition into this new job has been made significantly easier because of you!"

Alexandra smiled, "Thank you Rena Briellen. Once again, welcome! I am really looking forward to working with you."

As Alexandra concluded their conversation and headed back to her office on the ninth floor, Rena felt more relaxed because many of her previous initial reservations and looming questions had been addressed by Alexandra, such as:
- Where can I get help if I'm struggling?
- Who can I ask questions about my job or about the company?
- How can I learn about our company's culture and office politics[7]?

Although these were just a few of the many questions she had had, she now felt a greater sense of ease as she prepared for her first meeting with Freddie Nolen, who would be her immediate supervisor.

---

[6]This technique, taught by Danise DiStasi is utilized at the beginning of all meetings and interactions to set a positive tone.

[7]https://www.talmundo.com/blog/82-questions-your-new-hires-wishyoud-answer

Legislation

Establishing the basic groundwork for the mentoring relationship is a key element for success. That is legislation! You give yourself and your mentoring partner an advantage by **legislating a mentoring agreement** at the beginning of the relationship, so as to provide a concrete foundation for what both mentor and mentee desire to accomplish throughout the mentoring relationship. It also helps both mentor and mentee to manage relational expectations by clearly defining their respective commitments. Ultimately, a well-crafted agreement **provides the framework for the scope of the relationship**, and acts as a contract between the mentee and mentor[8].

The Beginning of the End?

It was two-o-clock when Alexandra looked up from the financial projections that she had been working on. She had put a notification alert on her calendar to check back with Rena to go over their mentoring contract, and it was at that moment that she heard a faint knock on her office door. "Come in!" Alexandra's warm voice was a comfort to Rena's ears, but, unfortunately, Rena looked as if someone had taken the wind out of her sails. "How is it going Rena?" Alexandra asked with a heightened tone of concern.

"Alexandra, I am exhausted, upset, frustrated, disillusioned, disgruntled, distressed and discouraged – and it is only my first day!" Rena paused for a second to catch her breath. "Should I keep going?"

Alexandra, who was in the midst of year-end earnings projections, was

[8]Laura Francis. https://www.riversoftware.com/mentor-menteeadvice/mentoring-agreements/

completely caught off guard. Even though she remained poker faced, she thought to herself, "Oh crap, what have I gotten into this time? It is way too early for this!"

"Rena, wow! What happened? It has only been a couple of hours since I saw you last!"

After the initial shock, Alexandra was genuinely concerned about her new mentee's well-being. It had only been a short time since they parted ways in the morning, but she could see that Rena was flustered and visibly distraught.

"Look Alexandra, this morning, even from our short conversation, I feel like I can trust you, so I am going to be frank and honest. I know it is very early, and I am risking a lot by sharing this with you." Rena took a deep breath. "I am not sure that Strategion is going to be the right place for me," Rena blurted out. "I met Freddie, my immediate supervisor, and we hit it off immediately. He is an incredibly emotionally intelligent person. I thought that I would be very excited to work for him. But, during our team meeting, I definitely did not get the same vibe back from Freddie's team."

In response to Rena's comments, Alexandra's eyebrows raised. She definitely was not expecting her new protégé to have issues on the first day. "Really? What happened?" Alexandra continued. Rena wasn't sure what can of worms she was opening, and, inwardly, she hoped that her exterior did not betray the anxiety that had settled in the pit of her stomach like leftover pizza.

Rena cautiously continued, "Freddie introduced me to the team at the beginning of the marketing meeting. Everyone went around the room and shared cordial well wishes and smiles, and then the real meeting began. I quickly realized that my marketing team was in the midst of a civil war with regard to the roll-out of Strategion's new marketing strategy."

Alexandra nodded slowly. She personally knew the head of the marketing department, but was not familiar with most of the managers and staff that would become Rena's team.

Rena continued, "After my brief welcome and introduction, the meeting quickly turned ugly as several of the other managers became visibly frustrated with their colleagues who had opposed the first draft of their marketing strategy. Even though I sat like a fly on the wall, it was not long before the frustrated managers put me on the spot and asked me to sign-off on their half-baked plan. Everyone in the meeting turned and looked at me – expecting me to give my opinion! I was caught completely off guard."

"How did you respond?" Alexandra was transfixed. The finance department had never had such drama.

Rena replied, "I was mortified. Like a deer in headlights. I had no idea what to say! So, I said nothing! Thank goodness, Freddie jumped in the middle and called off the wolves. He told them that I needed time to review the plan and marketing strategy before I would be able to make an informed decision. Freddie even apologized for the contentious nature of his colleagues."

Alexandra, utilizing her newly-acquired listening techniques, leaned in and repeated Rena's statement, "So, Freddie told them that you needed time to review the plan and marketing strategy?"

"Yes. I really did not have enough time to make an informed decision, and I honestly felt like they were simply trying to get me to take sides. I felt like it was completely unfair and very unprofessional. I can't afford to make any enemies." Rena stared out the window and continued to reflect. "Especially on my first day!"

"How do you feel now?" Alexandra wanted to make sure that Rena did not feel rushed, even though her projection deadlines were staring her in the face.

"To be completely honest with you, Alexandra, I am kind of torn. I must admit that I did not expect to be thrust into a crash course on office politics and water-cooler alliances on my first day. I am also feeling a little anxious because I am not sure what it says about the company's culture. Even though Freddie stood up for me, I am still wondering if I made the right choice."

Alexandra thoughtfully pondered her next response. She wanted Rena to know that she was listening and that their mentor-mentee relationship was going to be a safe haven for honest discussion and authentic feedback.

"I feel that all of your emotions are valid, justified, and definitely warranted at this juncture," replied Alexandra, making sure to maintain eye contact. She did not want Rena to feel as if her responses were coming from a textbook. "I also feel that your response was perfect. It is obvious that the team is somewhat fragmented, and that they are trying to build alliances and suck you in. I know it's early in our relationship, but I want to celebrate you for your professionalism and decorum. Remaining neutral will immediately gain respect for you, and show your team that you can think for yourself."

"Do you really think I responded correctly?" Rena pressed, "Please be honest with me."

"Yes, I think you responded appropriately." Alexandra, speaking decisively, continued, "And, should you choose to stay at Strategion, I think you are going to do very well here. I am humbled that you trusted me enough to share your concerns. This will always be a safe space." Smiling, she continued, "Hopefully, I will see you tomorrow morning. I will send you a calendar invite this afternoon, but we will meet first thing in the morning to LEGISLATE our mentoring contract, schedule our ongoing mentoring meetings, and keep it moving. Let me know what you like in your coffee."

The Pre-Game Conference

The "Pre-Game Conference" or "Preliminary Briefing[9]" is an intentionally scheduled meeting where the mentor and mentee LEGISLATE specific goals and objectives that will serve as the parameters and guidelines for the mentor-mentee engagement. During this very important meeting, both parties will

---

[9]The terms are interchangeable and can be substituted in favor of a wide range of names, all of which should signify the initial meetings between mentor and mentee that outline the specifics of the mentoring engagement.

define the length of the engagement, and the frequency and length of their mentoring sessions.

Both the mentee and mentor should take a proactive stance to articulate and list their unique expectations. Another critical component of the legislative briefing includes the mentor assisting and supporting the mentee as he/she sets S.M.A.R.T. goals:

S – SPECIFIC
M – MEASURABLE
A – ATTAINABLE
R – RELEVANT
T – TIME-BOUND

These S.M.A.R.T. goals serve as critical guideposts and yard-sticks to measure the effectiveness of the mentoring relationship.

Opening Day Again

"Good Morning, Rena! I'm glad that you decided to come back today!" Alexandra's office was filled with the distinct aroma of a gourmet Kenyan coffee blend. The smell reminded Rena of her semester abroad. "Let me begin, again, by saying, congratulations, and I am genuinely excited for you and your career. After the events of yesterday, I really am glad that you decided to come back today. As you know, Strategion assigned me as your mentor based upon our similar interests, temperaments, career path and personality inventory."

Rena swiveled in Alexandra's comfortable office chair, lifted the cup of coffee to her nose, and breathed in the distinct fragrance of the high Kenyan plateau.

Alexandra continued, "Let's begin with a simple question. Can you tell me something positive that has happened in your life? It can be personal or professional."

Rena smiled, saying, "Didn't you ask me the same question yesterday?"

"I sure did, but today is a new day, and today will require a new positive outlook, so I am all ears. What do you have?" Alexandra sat back in her chair and smiled while taking a sip of the gourmet roast.

 "Ok, on my commute to work I wanted to prepare for our meeting today, so I began listening to a podcast about SMART goals. I learned that SMART goals are critical to keep the ball moving forward for personal and professional development."

"I also learned that having a mentor is a powerful asset to assist in accomplishing those goals!" Rena winked and lifted her cup of coffee in Alexandra's direction. "Cheers!"

Alexandra laughed. "Rena! You are awesome!"

"Thanks for being willing to share." Alexandra continued, "After a day like yesterday, I think this is the perfect opportunity to LEGISLATE our mentoring contract, lay some ground rules, review our expectations, and set some ambitious but realistic goals for our first year together. We must be sure to include quarterly benchmarks, and a mid-year assessment to make sure that we are both satisfied with our course. After we complete our agreement, we will sign and submit a copy to our HR department for an additional layer of accountability. It will also give you a legal document should any problems arise. What do you think?"

"Sounds good. Let's get started," said Rena, breathing another sigh of relief.

Alexandra pulled out Strategion's template, handed a copy to Rena, and they both then began typing notes on their laptops.

Strategion's Mentee/Mentor Agreement Template

1. **Length of mentoring commitment**
2. **Explicit parameters for the termination of the mentoring relationship**
3. **Length and frequency of mentoring meetings**
4. **Specific S.M.A.R.T. goals**
5. **Specific means of accountability**
6. **Preferred methods and frequency of communication**
7. **Contact Information of Program Supervisor**
8. **Confidentiality Clause**
9. **Signatures**

"Ok Rena, first of all, you are going to have to put up with me for one whole year! That is the length of Strategion's mentoring program. By this time next year, you will probably be mentoring me!" Alexandra smiled. "Strategion will have a gala at the end of the year to celebrate our achievements and accomplishments[10]."

Alexandra continued, "Strategion also recommends that we meet monthly; however, they leave that up to us – based upon our respective work schedules. How often would you like to connect?"

Rena started in, "I was thinking about yesterday, and how beneficial it was to connect with you. I promise that I won't harass you with each crisis that I face, but is it possible that we could initially meet weekly for the first month, and then less frequent as I settle into my routine?"

---

[10]Successful corporate mentoring programs incorporate periodic celebrations to observe the accomplishments of mentors and mentees in their programs.

"I am ok with that. Does a weekly thirty minute check-in work for you?" Alexandra asked. "That would be awesome. As you know, my schedule is pretty open, so please let me know your availability so that I can put it on my calendar." Rena was excited.

"Ok, I proposed that we make our meeting times consistent so that there is no confusion, and we are not tempted to reschedule." Alexandra knew that she needed regularly scheduled appointments on her calendar in order to prepare sufficiently.

Rena successfully typed in the parameters of the length and frequency of their meetings. She also included her preliminary list of S.M.A.R.T. goals. Rena and Alexandra agreed that they would check in with each other on a weekly basis, and would review Rena's goals on a monthly basis for accountability. Rena sent the document to the printer, and a hard copy was signed by both Rena and Alexandra. Strategion had stipulated that the mentee was responsible for completing the mentoring agreement template, and submitting a copy of the document to HR.

The Second Meeting

For the second mentor-mentee meeting, Strategion provided all of its mentors with a mentoring article that outlined the Five C's[11] for their protégé's performance and personal life. The Five C's constituted a powerful framework of objectives to guide the mentor-mentee agreement and subsequent interactions.

- Your Core - personality assessments, personal presentation, interpersonal communication, interpersonal relationships
- Your Craft - developing functional skill, vocational and technical ability, occupation specific skill set, and on-the-job training
- Your Career - charting career growth, goals, strategies, and organizational hierarchy
- Your Community -defining and becoming an involved community contributor

- Your Compartments - maintaining work-life balance, managing life changes, dealing with competing demands"

Alexandra sent the article to Rena in preparation for their second meeting.

"Wow that sounds pretty comprehensive!" Rena remarked. "I did not expect the program to be so structured."

"Yes, upon a comprehensive study, our company has concluded that the most successful mentoring programs are developed and implemented with a focused structure that requires its mentees to be the proactive innovators in the goal-setting process. In other words, this means, Rena, that you must be the one who determines our curriculum, and the one who narrows our focus so that you will receive the maximum benefit and personal satisfaction."

Mentoring Roles

Alexandra continued, "Another cool element within Strategion's Mentor Training Module is their explanation of the various roles that mentors can play throughout the mentoring process.

These are very similar to the famous mentors who appear in our favorite movies (like Mr. Miyagi in Karate Kid, Dumbledore in Harry Potter, Gandalf in Lord of the Rings, or even M, played by Judi Dench in recent James Bond movies). These are the character roles that Strategion encourages its mentors to become familiar with. I thought it would be cool to share these roles with you. More than likely, you will relate to some of the roles better than others. Check these out!"

Alexandra handed Rena a laminated 8.5 by 11 sheet of paper entitled, "Mentoring Roles." Rena did a quick perusal and took in the information.

Alexandra laughed when Rena said, "It looks like Strategion expects me to play these roles over the entire next year!"

[11]This is an adaptation of Qualcomm's Mentorship Toolkit's "The Five Mys"

1. LION-ATHENA – *The Process Partner*

"The Helper of Heroes" (Athens has the goddess of wisdom, courage, inspiration, civilization, law and justice, strategic warfare, mathematics, strength, strategy, the arts, crafts, and other skills). Assists the mentee with creating a strategy and specific plan for achieving their goals[12.]

2. OWL-SOCRATES – *The Thought Partner*

Socrates's style of teaching — immortalized as "The Socratic Method" — involved not conveying knowledge, but, rather, asking question after clarifying question until his students arrived at their own understandings; here, assisting the mentee with refining their skills and professional development by asking questions and listening.

3. GOLDEN RETRIEVER - PLATO –*The Performance Partner*

Assisting the mentee to discover solutions to improve their performance and continue their development – resulting in their best self by uniquely, unconditionally, and powerfully assisting the mentee with converting feedback into action. The mentor acts as a loyal supporter, and a cheerleader, and always expresses unconditional positive regard[13] (See Chapter [8].)

---

[12]Athena (Latin: Minerva) is the goddess of wisdom, war strategy, and arts and crafts. Often shown bearing a shield depicting the gorgon Medusa (Aegis) given to her by her father Zeus. Athena is an armed warrior goddess, and appears in Greek mythology as a helper of many heroes, including Hercules, Jason, and Odysseus.

[13]Plato, the ancient Greek philosopher was a protégé of Socrates and a mentor to Aristotle. Plato is best known as the author of philosophical works of unparalleled influence. Plato's works contain discussion in aesthetics, political philosophy, ethics, theology, cosmology, epistemology, and the philosophy of language. Founder of the Academy in 380, Plato is credited with establishing the ultimate ancestor of the modern university. Constance C. Meinwald, Professor of Philosophy, University of Illinois, Chicago.

4. **EAGLE - MORPHEUS**–The Vision Partner
Always creates a "safe and trusting" relationship – allowing
the mentee to dream and envision greater realities, and
assisting the mentee with branching out, having new
experiences, and meeting others to expand their professional
network[14.] (See chapter nine on Launching).

Alexandra concluded, "Over the course of the next year, you will interact
with all four of these roles. Some days, I will show up as Socrates, like a wise
old owl, questioning and inquiring about your motives, actions, and
decisions.

Rena nodded. She was not aware that mentoring was such a sophisticated
undertaking.

"Other days, I will arrive as Eagle-Eyed Morpheus - an advocate for your
dreams, visions, and the many great possibilities that await you. At any rate,
these are the roles in which I will operate over the next twelve months."

Alexandra paused to see if the conversation was registering with Rena.
"What are you thinking?" she asked Rena.

"The more you talk, the more intrigued I become! Now, I am not sure if a
weekly check-in will be sufficient! I probably will need to talk to you every
day! Just kidding, but not really!"

Rena was excited to finally have an experienced guide to help her navigate the
journey ahead. Even though her undergraduate education had provided her
with a strategy for the progression of her career, Rena had always felt like it
was cookie cutter. She had desperately longed for a mentor who would have
the ability to coach, advise, and share in her goals and dreams.

---

[14]Morpheus of Greco-Roman mythology was known as the god of dreams.

Brushstrokes

It is imperative during the "legislative process", that the mentor provides the space for her/his protégé to shape the curriculum, the goals, and the structure of the mentoring engagement. By allowing the protégé to determine their specific areas of concentration and personal development, the protégé will take ultimate responsibility for their growth and progress.

Meanwhile, the mentor's responsibility is to serve as a faithful guide and companion as the mentee selects various roads, paths, and alleys to traverse. Remember, effective mentoring is an art!

CHAPTER TWO

LEAVING

Every formal mentoring relationship should begin with the end in mind in order to designate how the mentor-protégé match will terminate, to establish clear boundaries, and to prevent unnecessary pain and frustration.

"Mentorships, similar to other important relationships, usually end. Ideological differences and a need to chart a personal path might preclude parties from maintaining the original balance that stabilized a mentoring relationship. Conflict between an apprentice and his master is not always bad; in fact, it is almost inevitable if the apprentice's destiny is to exceed the accomplishments of the master."
- Kilroy J. Oldster

"Abandonment doesn't have the sharp but dissipating sting of a slap. It's like a punch to the gut, bruising your skin, and driving the precious air from your body."
- Tayari Jones

"Parting is such sweet sorrow that I shall say goodnight till it be morrow."
- Shakespeare

Meet Shawn the Mentee

Being employed by a Fortune 500 company is never easy, but the last two years had been exceptionally difficult for Shawn Richards. Although he had been hired to head his company's growing IT department, he (and the rest of the executive team) had been completely blindsided by the Board of Director's decision to purchase two additional startups in the same year. Looking back with a sense of pride, Shawn realized that, as one of the youngest CIOs in Silicon Valley, he had successfully navigated his company through the deep and turbulent waters of a corporate merger, and had emerged with a reputation for excellence and the nickname **"Inartificial Intelligence."**

However, as he was sitting at his desk, Shawn got a queasy feeling in his gut when he thought about what the next phase of his career should look like. Due to his humble beginnings, he had a deep internal motivation to be financially successful. On the other hand, he also had the irrefutable desire to leave a legacy that transcended his personal balance sheet.

In a conversation over lunch, Shawn began to confide in one of the members of his executive team, Sheila Rowan, about the need to receive guidance and sage advice from someone who had already navigated the waters of the volatile and ever-expanding field of information technology. "There has got to be someone who understands the complexity of our industry, but who would be comfortable enough in their own skin not to view me as competition or a threat!"

"What do you mean?" Sheila pressed for more details.

Shawn paused in pensive introspection and then continued, "Every CEO or CIO that I have met is so narcissistic and territorial. All of them have immediately dismissed me as a novice because of my age, or thought that I was an ambitious brat who was trying to take their position. It is so disheartening because all I want is some honest, unbiased feedback so that I can feel more secure in my career decisions."

Sheila could sense Shawn's frustration, and genuinely wanted to help. "Shawn, I just read about an executive coaching company located just outside of Nashville that specializes in connecting young executives like yourself with more seasoned professionals. Maybe you should check it out. I have a 1:00 pm meeting, but I will send you the link to their website when I get back to my desk. The article specifically mentioned a coaching guru named Troy Robbs. Let me know when you have made contact with him."

Shawn nodded at this point. He was definitely open to all suggestions.

Mentoring Meeting

Troy Robbs, the Executive Director of Executive Mentoring Solutions (EMS) was genuinely excited to hear about the incredible path that Shawn's career had taken. Their initial phone interview lasted well over an hour, as they talked back and forth about the challenges of corporate culture, the complexities of entrepreneurship, and starting one's own company.

Shawn was overwhelmed with excitement when Troy expressed a desire to connect him with a seasoned executive who had tentatively agreed to a year-long mentoring relationship. Chief Information Officer for a well-known tech giant, Anderson Cruse appeared to embody every quality that a successful IT executive could possess. He was intelligent, meticulous, innovative, enterprising, and idiosyncratic (in a good way). Shawn could see himself immediately advancing his career.

Match Meeting

As standard practice, Troy Robbs arranged and facilitated the initial mentor-mentee match meeting. Sitting at a restaurant on Nashville's music row, the three of them shared introductions, and Troy recommended that Shawn and Anderson spend a significant amount of time crafting and discussing their mentor agreement. Troy encouraged them to be very frank and explicit with regard to their expectations and intended outcomes by providing them with a template of questions to consider and a standard form to complete.

Troy also challenged Shawn and Anderson to spend an equally significant time specifically devoted to goal setting. Knowing Shawn's situation and concerns, Troy provided them with a list of sample SMART goals to get the ball rolling. At the conclusion of the initial mentor/mentee match meeting, Troy had Anderson and Shawn sign a standard intake form with their contact information, and the basic details of the mentoring agreement.

Troy concluded the meeting with, "Thanks gentlemen. I am excited about the upcoming year! It is very important that, once you complete the specific details of your agreement – such as frequency of your meetings, preferred methods of communication, expectations, and goals - that you send me the signed copy to keep in my files. This will serve as a guiding document for my quarterly reviews. Do you have any questions?"

Shawn and Anderson nodded. The three exchanged handshakes, and the adventure began.

Mentoring Meeting #2

The next face-to-face meeting between Shawn Richards and Anderson Cruse was specifically dedicated to LEGISLATING the details of the mentoring agreement. Shawn and Anderson worked out the specifics of their mentoring agreement to include the usual goals, check-in points, meeting times, and expectations. Shawn and Anderson were careful to include specific parameters to ensure that the mentoring relationship would produce mutual benefits and rewards. Their final draft looked like the following:

Mentor-Mentee Agreement

The Mentoring Agreement is created to ensure that mentors and mentees develop a mutual understanding of expectations from the beginning of their relationship. Additionally, it creates a series of identifiable benchmarks and goals to work toward and to use to evaluate progress. The following agreement is made between

....
Anderson Cruse-Mentor

....
Shawn Richards-Mentee

We are voluntarily entering into this mentoring relationship which we both want to be a productive and rewarding experience. To minimize the possibility of confusion, we have agreed to the following:

Confidentiality. All information and content shared between the Mentor and the Mentee shall remain confidential in perpetuity unless/until the parties agree to the contrary.

Expectations. It is expected that the Mentor will provide educational and development advice and guidance, and that both parties will work together to identify the Mentee's personal and professional goals, as well as to develop a plan for achieving those goals.

Meetings. The Mentee and the Mentor will meet and talk at least _____ minutes at a time and at a place that is mutually agreed upon. Meeting times, once agreed upon, should not be cancelled, unless it is unavoidable. Meetings that are cancelled should be rescheduled as soon as possible. At the end of each meeting, the Mentor and Mentee will agree on a date for the next meeting.

Each meeting will last a minimum of _____ minutes and a maximum of _____ minutes.

Length of Relationship. Mentoring relationships vary in length depending on circumstances. Our goal at Executive Mentoring Services (EMS) is to maintain our relationship for at least one year, at which time an evaluation will take place to determine the efficacy of the relationship. However, either party has the option of discontinuing the relationship for any reason, provided the terminating party notifies the other.

Additional Agreements

We agree that the role of the Mentor is to:

....

....

We agree that the role of the Mentee is to:

....

....

The Mentor agrees to be honest and provide constructive feedback while sharing insight on their own experiences as well. The Mentee agrees to be open to feedback that the Mentor shares in addition to providing constructive recommendations for the mentor.

Mentor's Signature...Date:...............

Mentee's Signature...Date: ....

With all of the forms and formalities completed, the thought of finally having a brain to pick, produced a giddiness in Shawn that he had not experienced since he landed his first job out of college. He truly felt that the relationship would provide the much-needed impetus to get out of his current career depression, and propel him to the next level of corporate executive leadership

Mentoring Meltdown

After just a few short weeks, Shawn noticed that Anderson had become increasingly harder to reach. Unanswered text messages, unanswered emails, and unreturned calls began to affect their communication. Trying not to take Anderson's elusiveness personally, Shawn continued to reach out in an attempt to remain proactive. Also, he kept a copy of their mentoring agreement on his desk because he wanted to be able to refer to it whenever he felt that he needed a "refresher" of the specific contents to make sure that he remained a man of his word. Frustrated, disgruntled, disappointed, and hurt, Shawn reached out to Troy Robbs to inquire about Anderson's mental status and general situation.

Troy's concern was evident. "I am really sorry to hear about this. Let me do some investigative work and get back with you. I will call you within forty-eight hours with a response."

Two days later, as promised, Troy reached out to Shawn.
"Shawn, I think I've got some bad news," Troy explained.
Shawn could sense that this was not going to end well. "Yes, Troy, I'm listening."

"I did some research, and it looks like Anderson was recently offered a new position in Seattle. I am not certain, but I would assume that, over the last several weeks, he has been extremely busy packing and going through the logistics of relocation. I'm sorry. I am still trying to reach out to him so that I can meet up directly with him and talk."

"Wow. Really? That's so unprofessional of him to just ghost me like that!

Why didn't he return my calls?" Shawn was incensed.

Troy could hear the disappointment and angst in Shawn's voice. New jobs and relocations were commonplace in his many years as an Executive Coach, but he had never encountered a situation quite like this one.

"I apologize, Shawn. I'm really stumped, and I admit that I am just as surprised as you are." Troy's wheels were spinning.

 Troy continued, "Shawn, can you stop by my office when you have some time?" Troy was treading lightly. He continued, "I would love to help you debrief and discuss our next steps."

Shawn was a little ambivalent about Troy's well-meaning request. Admittedly, he was still reeling from the emotional trauma of feeling rejected and abandoned. No one likes rejection, not even CIOs of Fortune 500 companies, he thought to himself.

Troy continued, "I will send your admin several calendar invites for next week so that you can pick the best time to come in. I would like to move quickly on this." After a moment's hesitation, Shawn agreed. "Ok, I will see you next week."

Picking Up The Pieces

Shawn walked into the lobby of Executive Mentoring Services and sat on the big brown leather sofa. Grazing through the magazines, he realized that his hands were shaking, and his heart was still racing. He simply could not get beyond the events of the past week. Specifically, he was having a difficult time resolving the fact that he had allowed himself to become excited and emotionally attached to the prospect of finally having a mentor to help him navigate the many questions regarding his career.

Troy Robbs came to the lobby and asked Shawn to step back to his office. "I really appreciate you coming in. I know this has been a difficult couple of days."

Shawn nodded, "Indeed it has."

Troy attempted to keep it light, "Can I get you a cup of coffee?"

"I'm good. Thanks, though," replied Shawn as he followed Troy from the reception area back to his office. The Nashville foliage was beautiful at this time of the year.

As Troy opened the door to his office, Shawn was visibly shaken when Anderson Cruse met him at the door.

Troy started in, "Shawn, I really felt...." but Anderson interrupted Troy mid-sentence: "Shawn, Troy explained to me how critical our mentoring arrangement is. He reminded me of my written commitment and the year-long pledge that I had made to you. I want to apologize for allowing my circumstances to cloud my judgment. I know that our relationship carries significant weight, and I again apologize for the great amount of emotional anguish I have caused you. Would you have me back?"

Shawn was conflicted. He didn't know whether to respond in a rage, and let Anderson have a piece of his mind, or to jump up and down in excitement.

Anderson continued, "Before you respond, I want you to know that Troy and I have discussed what a "remote mentoring" arrangement would look like utilizing video conferencing. In addition, Troy and I both agreed to fully fund four quarterly visits out to Seattle in order for us to fulfill our in-person meeting quota as is stated in our original mentoring agreement."

Anderson paused, hoping that Shawn could sense his genuine desire to make things right.

[**Every mentoring organization should pride itself on best-practices and abiding by national mentoring standards. One of those mentoring standards is closure. Mentoring organizations must take great care to prevent mentoring relationships from ending in a potentially damaging manner.**]

Troy jumped in, "On a personal note, I was so distraught about your situation that I flew out to Seattle after our meeting last week to have a personal conversation with Anderson. I don't say that to pat myself on the back or to seek your approval, but to show you how committed we both are to your personal and professional development. As you know, trust is the foundation to every mentoring relationship, and it is my hope that you will trust again."

Troy paused for a moment to assess Shawn's reaction. After a few moments of awkward silence, Troy had to make a conscious decision not to start talking again. He knew that Shawn was thinking, and he did not want to fill the awkward silence with unnecessary banter that might interrupt the young executive's pensive reflection.

Shawn finally broke the silence, "I really appreciate the fact that you both thought enough of me to schedule this meeting. Anderson, I am grateful that you took the time out of your busy schedule to fly here from Seattle. I am truly ecstatic about the next phase in your career and all of the opportunities that could potentially open up as a result."

Anderson smiled and graciously nodded. He could tell that, despite his feelings, Shawn was doing everything within him to employ professionalism, decorum and diplomacy.

Shawn continued, "Troy, I am also appreciative of the great lengths that you went through to help me out. Not only have you been a source of encouragement, you and the members of your staff have consistently shown professionalism and excellent customer service throughout this process."

"Thank you, Shawn," Troy replied.

"All that being said, I have decided to take a couple of months to do a little soul-searching. As I stated, I am appreciative of both of your efforts; however, I would like to step back and take some time to reflect and determine why I allowed this process to have such a paralyzing effect on my performance. I want to be better prepared for facing disappointment and unmet expectations."

Anderson had not expected Shawn's response, but he nodded in acquiescence.

Shawn stood up, hugged Troy, and then stretched his hand in Anderson's direction. "Would it be possible to reconnect with both of you in a couple of months? Maybe at that time, we can assess our current situations and potentially pick up where we left off?"

The importance of closure should never be minimized. Mentoring relationships should always begin with the end in mind.

INTEGRATION

Begin With The End in Mind

Since this is just the second chapter, to many, it would seem illogical to have a discussion about the end of the mentoring relationship. But at this juncture, it is critically important for every mentor and mentoring organization to understand the vital and foundational concept of closure – both planned and unplanned.

Unplanned closure occurs when there is conflict between the mentor and mentee, between the mentor and parent, when rules have been broken, when one party ends communication with the other, when there is an unexpected health or family issue, or when someone has to move unexpectedly. Because of the powerful emotional connection that often accompanies the mentoring relationship, strong emotions are involved with closure. All parties involved have the potential to feel a great sense of loss, sadness, betrayal, depression, catharsis, relief, anger, happiness, or even confusion when the mentoring relationship comes to an end. Discussing closure at the outset and during the mentoring engagement vastly increases the likelihood that the mentor and protégé leave the relationship in a healthy manner and in a positive frame of mind.

As we jump into the second chapter, keep in mind that Steven Covey's second habit of highly effective persons is to begin with the end in mind. It means "to begin each day, task or project with a clear vision of your desired direction and destination." This is especially critical in the mentoring arena. In fact, MENTOR has defined "closure" as one of the six elements of effective practice for mentoring.

There is a familiar equation that provides a quick glimpse into any relationship's success:

$$E - R = D$$

In other words, Expectations Minus Reality Equals Disappointment
This simple mathematical equation is the easiest way to describe the emotions that each of us experience when someone or something does not live up to our preconceived notions or expectations. This equation especially rings true in the context of interpersonal relationships. In fact, most relationships end because one of the parties has been dissatisfied, disillusioned, disheartened, or disappointed in the other party's performance. It goes without saying that the mentoring relationship is no different. Consequently, to avoid disappointment, it is imperative that both the mentor and mentee are able to identify and articulate their expectations as they head into their mentoring engagement.

Common Mentor Expectations

Mentors often bring their own set of expectations into the mentoring relationship. A few of these are:
- Mentors expect mentees to take initiative in the relationship
- Mentors expect mentees to be honest
- Mentors expect mentees to invest in the relationship

Common Mentee Expectations

Mentees bring their own unique set of expectations to the mentoring relationship. A few of these are:
- Mentees expect mentors to take time out of their schedule to connect
- Mentees expect mentors to listen and express genuine concern
- Mentees expect praise and encouragement from their mentors
- Mentees expect honest feedback

Common Parent Expectations

When mentoring youth, it is important that the parents' expectations are articulated and discussed. A few typical parental expectations:
- Parents expect mentors to consistently meet with the mentee
- Parents expect to be kept in the loop in the event of unforeseen situations
- Parents expect the mentee to engage with the mentor

How To Begin With The End in Mind

Mentoring relationships, like all other relationships, come to an end at some point. The issue is not necessarily the fact THAT THEY END, but HOW THEY END. As a mentoring relationship ends, it has the potential to serve as a launchpad for career growth, academic achievement, and emotional and interpersonal efficacy. On the other hand, as in Shawn's case, the ending of a mentoring relationship can result in a crippling source of pain and frustration. Similarly, in many youth mentoring programs, the unexplained loss of a mentor can be devastating.

It is here that we must maintain a vigilant eye to ensure that our mentees are the recipients of an empowering, encouraging, enlightening, and educating mentoring engagement.

Bringing a mentoring relationship to closure in a way that affirms the contributions of both the mentor and the mentee is essential to ensuring that the relationship ends with positive consequences for the mentee. Closure is a normal stage in a mentoring relationship, and mentors and mentees should be able to prepare for closure in addition to providing valuable personal and professional feedback with regard to the efficacy of the mentoring engagement.

Brushstrokes

- Here are a few concepts for mentors, corporate mentoring programs, and youth-based mentoring organizations to consider with regard to facilitating healthy closure within the context of each mentoring engagement.

- Be clear and honest about closure
- Give mentees an adequate amount of time to prepare for when the last meeting will take place
- Be intentional about discussing feelings and emotions that result from ending relationships
- Help the mentee reflect and celebrate progress
- Discuss positive memories and events of the relationship
- Provide mentee with parting advice and words of wisdom

- Recognize mentors and mentees at company outings and meetings

When crafting the **initial mentoring agreement**, all parties involved must take time to assess how long the mentoring engagement will last, and how it will come to a close. Because closure or termination is a very normal and expected stage of every mentoring relationship, it is best practice to layout the parameters for a smooth and efficacious conclusion. *MENTOR* recommends various closure activities, such as year-end celebrations, award ceremonies, exit interviews, and match meetings. During these closing activities, care should be taken to allocate time for positive and constructive reflection. Moments of reflection almost always provide opportunities for growth, and often mitigate negative experiences. In addition, mentors, mentoring agencies, and human resource offices can provide mentees/protégés with **post-agreement "next steps"** to ensure that the mentor continues his/her personal and professional growth plan.

Once again, the importance of closure should never be minimized. Thus, **mentoring relationships should always begin with the end in mind.**

CHAPTER THREE

LABORING

The mentor and mentee must work diligently to ensure the success of the mentoring relationship.

"A dream does not become reality through magic; it takes sweat, determination, and hard work."
- Colin Powell, former U.S. Defense Secretary

"I have learned that success is to be measured not so much by the position that one has reached in life, as by the obstacles which he has had to overcome while trying to succeed."
- Booker T. Washington, Educator and Presidential Advisor

"You may encounter many defeats, but you must not be defeated. In fact, it may be necessary to encounter the defeats, so you can know who you are, what you can rise from, and how you can still come out of it."
- Maya Angelou

Meet Isaiah, the Mentee

As I got out of my car and headed to the office, the sedan in the parking lot speeding toward me should have been a sign. Nevertheless, I stopped and paused to see what was going on.

The car quickly and abruptly turned into one of the parking spaces, and the driver's side door violently swung open. A young, professional woman in her late-thirties sprung out of the car, and immediately slammed the door behind her. She came around to the passenger's side, pounded on the window, and yelled, "Come on, boy!"

Not wanting to be awkward or appear nosey, I continued to walk ever so slowly toward my office building, occasionally glancing to observe the heated exchange in the parking lot. Slowly, the passenger door opened, and a young teenager emerged. It was obvious that he was being forced to a meeting, and he was passively aggressively sabotaging all of his mother's intentions.

Ms. Minor walked hurriedly toward the front door of my office building while her son, about thirty paces behind her, walked slowly, painfully, and laboriously in her wake. It was incredibly obvious that she was far beyond her wit's end. Mom looked frazzled, frantic, flabbergasted, and, frankly, fed up. But Isaiah looked worse, much worse. His tall lanky frame was accentuated by a bowed head and slumped shoulders. The young man's hair was unkempt, his clothes were disheveled, his shirt was untucked, his pants were wrinkled and stained, and his muddy shoes looked "worn" and untied.

However, it was not the young man's outward appearance that caused my eyebrows to raise. It was the mix of conflicting signals that emanated from his facial expressions and body language. Yes, the most obvious emotions were anger and defiance, but, as I looked deeper into Isaiah's eyes, I was not surprised to see the deeper feelings of betrayal, fear, sadness, and loneliness.

"Ms. Minor, it is great to finally meet you. I am glad you are here," I opened.

With no time for pleasantries, Ms. Minor jumped right in, "I'm glad we are here, too. I am so tired of fighting with that boy!" She glared at Isaiah, whose eyes remained transfixed on the floor. He seemed to embrace the notion that making eye contact would result in imminent danger. Meanwhile, Ms. Minor wasted no time going on and on as her frustration and disgust reverberated in my ears.

"Well, why don't we begin with introductions?" I attempted to keep the tone light.

Ms. Minor continued, "Well, my name is Jackie, and this is Isaiah. He is going into the ninth grade at Frederick Douglass. He is pleased to meet you."

I discreetly and politely interrupted, "Isaiah, I am quite sure that a powerful young man like yourself is able to introduce himself." I stood up and motioned Isaiah to follow suit. "My name is Mr. Mufasa, and I am the director for Lions and Leaders Mentoring Company," I said as I reached out and extended my hand.

Without uttering a syllable, his mother glared in Isaiah's direction as if to say, "You better not do anything stupid!"

 Without making eye contact, Isaiah sheepishly stood up, his six foot frame slowly unfurled, and he extended his hand in my direction. The resulting handshake reminded me of a room temperature bowl of leftover linguine. "My name is Isaiah," the teenager mumbled in an inaudible tone that could only be heard by a bat in a sound-proof studio.

"Speak up boy! Can't nobody hear you when you mumbling' like that," screeched Ms. Minor, whose frustration was quickly reaching a boiling point.

Reticent and obviously weakened from years of intense warfare with his

Mom, Isaiah attempted to strengthen the linguine-like handshake and increased his decibels by .0005 percent, "Hello Mr. Mufasa, my name is Isaiah."

I smiled inside, I surmised that in ten years Isaiah would be running his own company, "Nice to meet you, Isaiah! I heard that you are quite a good running back. I am looking forward to hearing about your future football career."

After the initial parent and mentee intake, Mom and Isaiah were oriented, and joined Lions and Leaders. Within a few weeks, a suitable mentor with similar background and interests was identified. Having gone through the mentor background screening process, mentee training, and background checks, the potential mentee was ready to be introduced to Ms. Jackie.

The parent-mentor meeting is always necessary to ensure that a good collaborative and cooperative relationship can exist between the parent and the mentor prior to the mentor being introduced to the mentee. Once an agreement and consensus has been reached between the parent and the potential mentor, the mentor-mentee meeting is scheduled. In this case, Joe was the Mentor, and Isaiah was the Mentee.

Meet Joe the Mentor
Isaiah's newly identified mentor, Joe Somers, III, was very anxious to meet his protégé, and the initial meeting went well. Facilitated by the program director for Lions to Leaders, both Isaiah and Joe were coached about the parameters of their mentor-mentee agreement, their individual responsibilities, the labor required, commitments, expectations, and their individual responsibilities. Their agreement was signed and witnessed, and the adventure began.

As with every mentoring relationship, despite all of the careful planning, meticulous preparation, and training, the mentor and mentee can never fully anticipate what will ensue. The vicissitudes of life always bring a level of uncertainty to one's existence, and this is doubly true for mentors. Consequently, the mentor should never enter the relationship with the assumption that it will be smooth sailing, or that there will not be rough waters ahead. Instead, **the mentor and mentee must both realize that every mentoring relationship will be fraught with LABOR. In fact, without LABOR, there can be no progress**. Ultimately, Joe and Isaiah's relationship proved that to be true for them.

When Joe and Isaiah first began their mentoring relationship, Isaiah, who hailed from a particularly challenging home life, was quite resistant to Joe's attempts for conversation. Every question posed by Joe was answered with a one-word response, a simple shoulder-shrug, or, even worse, the "blank stare of death." Isaiah's emotional walls were formidable, seemingly impenetrable, and often erected intentionally as an insidious attempt to passive aggressively frustrate Joe, and everyone else. Fortunately, Joe was not green to mentoring, and actually expected Isaiah's passive aggressive, and often manipulative, responses. Joe knew that, with consistent, patient interaction, Isaiah would eventually warm up over time.

LABOR: Ask Your Mentee Open-Ended Questions

Joe made it a point to consistently ask probing, open ended questions. The questions pushed Isaiah beyond his typical one-word responses, and eventually opened the door for actual conversation.
- How did you feel about that?
- How would you do things differently next time?
- I am curious about why you think...
- How does this impact / help / hurt your goal?
- What did you learn?

LABOR: Allow Your Mentee To Finish His Thoughts and Sentences Without Interruption

In addition, Joe focused on allowing Isaiah to think and to process concepts slowly. He made sure never to interrupt or finish Isaiah's sentences. Joe resisted the powerful urge to put words in Isaiah's mouth, or to assume what Isaiah was thinking.

LABOR: Embrace the Silence

At the outset of their mentoring relationship, Isaiah's silence was awkward. Initially, assuming that Isaiah was an introvert, Joe scrambled to fill each lull in conversation with light banter and small talk. But after a little research, Joe learned to embrace Isaiah's disinterested, and blah tendencies – realizing that his mentee's moments of silence were often attempts to collect his thoughts, and process the events of the moment.

After time and practice, Joe began to embrace the uncomfortable silence, which, in turn, allowed Isaiah to experience Joe's incredible patience and unconditional acceptance. Invariably, over the course of several months, Isaiah began to trust Joe as his mentor. He opened up, deeper conversations ensued, and their interactions began to flourish. Joe was pleasantly surprised to find out that **Isaiah was no introvert at all. He just needed a good listening ear!**

LABOR: Set Goals

At the beginning of Joe and Isaiah's mentoring relationship, Joe spent a considerable amount of time explaining to Isaiah the indispensable importance of setting goals. At the first goal-setting strategy meeting, Joe began by providing Isaiah with five categories for which to categorize his **S.M.A.R.T. goals:**

1.   Physical Goals
2.   Spiritual Goals
3.   Educational / Vocational Goals
4.   Relational Goals
5.   Financial Goals

After providing Isaiah with the five categories, Joe asked Isaiah a few simple questions for each goal:

- Where would you like to be PHYSICALLY by this time next year?
- How do you see yourself FINANCIALLY by this time next year?
- What do you want to accomplish SPIRITUALLY?
- What dreams do you have with regard to your physical ability?
- Schooling?
- Relationships?
- Fitness level?

Isaiah stared off into space, but Joe could tell that his little protégé's wheels were turning at a million miles per hour. At the age of fourteen, Isaiah, like most of his peers, aspired to play football in the National Football League. And, although his dream may have been far-fetched to some, Joe made a conscious decision not to dissuade him from his lofty goal, but, rather, to encourage Isaiah to give his best effort in the pursuit of ALL of his dreams – in addition to having a viable, well-thought-out option should he not get drafted by the Baltimore Ravens.

Isaiah's eyes lit up and sparkled as he began to speak. At the ripe-old age of fourteen, he had never had anyone express an interest in his aspirations. Up until this point, everyone had provided Isaiah with their self-imposed predeterminations of where he should devote his energy. All of his relatives and associates had thoroughly tried to convince him to give up on football, and to concentrate on something "more practical." He told Joe, "I want a 3.5 GPA, I want $500 in the bank, and I want to be able to bench 225 pounds. I want to be able to squat 315, and I want to be able to run a sub-5 40 yard dash, and have a six-pack."

"Is that all?" Joseph laughed sarcastically.

Isaiah continued, completely oblivious to Joe's sarcasm. He was in a zone. "That's all for now," Isaiah replied.

"Ok, let's break these goals down. Remember, we have to be very specific, and also develop a game plan to achieve each one!"

INTEGRATION
Getting In The Trenches: Goals and Growth

Over the course of the mentoring relationship, mentors should be prepared to LABOR diligently in two primary areas: goals and growth.

Laboring with GOALS

The establishment of a clear and consistent goal-setting strategy at the outset of the mentoring engagement is one of the elements that has the greatest potential to positively shape the performance of the mentee, and undergird the health of the mentor-mentee relationship.

The LABOR involved in establishing clear, quantifiable and attainable goals produces an exponential return on its initial time investment. Mentor Joe, Mentor Alexandra, and Mentor Anderson knew that, at the outset of their mentor engagement, they would have to spend a great deal of time hammering out their mentee's goal strategy. They knew that the goal strategy must be carefully executed with several key ingredients:

- Consistent Meetings,
- Accountability,
- Scheduled Benchmarks,
- Celebrations, and
- Frequent Course Corrections.

In the important process of setting goals, the mentor must carefully guide the mentee to envision his/herself in six months or a year – depending on the goal-setting period. Socratic, leading, open-ended questions are paramount for goal-setting discussions. For example:

- Where do you see yourself educationally in six months?
- Where do you see yourself relationally in six months?
- Where do you see yourself financially in six months?

These questions will ultimately form the basis for establishing specific, measurable, achievable, relevant, and time-stamped goals. From this discussion, a protégé can envision $5,000 in their bank account in six months, or having straight A's for the second quarter marking period.

Note: In the appendix the reader will find four positive results of the mentor / mentee relationship.

Laboring with GROWTH

Not only should mentors be willing to LABOR with their mentee's goals, but they should also be willing to LABOR with their mentee's growth – especially their character growth. **Great people are always judged by their character – not their money, not their prestige, position or pedigree.**

Having character means embodying such admirable traits as honesty, integrity, empathy, loyalty, cooperation, compassion, and generosity. At this juncture, it is beneficial for a mentor to understand his/her role as a model of character. Being honorable, honest, empathetic, and generous in the work that a mentor does, as well as in their relations with others, sets a good example for the mentee to follow.

When Joe began mentoring Isaiah, character formation, along with goal-setting, quickly became a primary concern. Joe had a strong desire to model these character strengths on a consistent basis in order to provide Isaiah with the internal strength and resilience necessary to thrive as an adult.

People with strong core values make the greatest contributions, have the best sense of self, form the most secure and healthy relationships, and build the strongest communities. They are also the happiest, and often feel gratified and successful in life. **People with strong character strengths are more resilient because they have the ability to return to a set of core values during trying times.** Essentially, such people know how to do the right thing, even when others are not looking.

Character strengths can roughly be divided into two groups — Performance Character Strengths and Moral Character Strengths.

Performance strengths predict success at school and work. They include qualities like tenacity, stick-to-it-ive-ness, and grit. **Moral character strengths** involve qualities like commitment to justice, fairness, and universal respect for others; they also include personal ways of interacting with people, such as always practicing generosity, forgiveness, honesty, caring, and loving kindness.

Moral character enables us to be resilient and to experience gratitude even during challenging moments. Both Joe the Mentor, and Alexandra the Mentor, proved to be excellent mentor models of performance and moral character. They also provided clear and consistent examples for Isaiah and Rena.

Brushstrokes

Reinforce the Positive

Telling your mentee how he/she should behave seldom works for parents, and this is doubly true for mentors. In fact, "preaching sessions" invariably backfire and undermine a mentee's trust and vulnerability. Instead, a mentor should intentionally seek to reinforce the positive behaviors of his/her mentee. Did your mentee display generosity? Humility? Kindness? Grit? If so, make it a point to acknowledge and honor the mentee's actions.

Rehearse the Empathy

Displaying empathy with one's mentee allows the mentor to live vicariously in the mentee's world, and experience the pain, the joy, and the broad spectrum of feelings that embody the mentee's existence. Mirroring the mentee's emotions and expressions show the mentee that his mentor is willing to engage and understand their perspective. Consequently, when the mentor models empathetic behavior, the mentee is able to understand the importance of empathy in all of their relationships.

Rejoice in the Improvement

None of us are perfect, and to expect our mentee to be perfect, frankly, would be hypocritical. As mentors, we should not expect our mentees to be perfect; however, we should expect our mentees to strive to make improvements, and improvements should always be celebrated. Rome was not built in a day, and everyone is striving to improve, including one's mentees.

Rally the Village

Another method of positively affecting a mentee's character development is to allow the mentee to meet and engage with the mentor's colleagues who possess character traits worthy of mention. (See also Chapter 9 – Lionizing) For example, consider a friend who continually embodies generosity, a co-worker who displays grit and perseverance on a project, or a relative who has an uncanny ability to listen empathetically. Your colleagues can be brought in as subject matter experts to have conversations with your mentee – thereby reinforcing positive character development.

Reward and Relish the Growth

Invariably, a mentor, will personally experience opportunities for their own character growth and development. Challenges at work and in relationships are often prime opportunities for a mentor to grow, and these events can productively be shared with mentees. Sharing such experiences with mentees often allows them to see the humanity and authentic character growth of their mentor.

As Joe and Isaiah walked out of the gym at the local community center, Isaiah noticed a crumpled up twenty dollar bill on the floor next to some vending machines. Isaiah immediately picked up the money and looked at Joe to see his reaction. Joe inquired, "What are you going to do with that?"

Isaiah looked at Joe intently, "At first, I was going to stick it in my pocket and keep it. However, after thinking about it, I am going to take it to the front desk and give it to the receptionist. Maybe someone dropped it by accident."

Joe replied, "Isaiah, I am so proud of you! Integrity is doing the right thing when no one is watching, and it takes a great deal of integrity to do what you just did."

Isaiah smiled, "Thanks, Mr. Joe!"

Joe reached in his wallet and handed Isaiah a twenty-dollar bill, "Character counts! Keep up the good work, young man!"

Artwork by Brandon Herbert

SECTION

PAINTING THE CANVAS

PAINTING THE CANVAS

The Principal Coat, consisting of the middle five chapters, will serve as the central focus of the book, and includes the essential methodology, techniques, and skills that are essential to mentor the next generation of leaders. Artists who sculpt call this stage Modeling.

In this section, we will delineate five best practices, and provide practical, grass-roots tips for developing and maintaining a successful mentoring relationship:

- LEADING
- LISTENING
- LEARNING
- LAUGHING
- LOVING

Chapter Four, LEADING encourages the mentor to artfully lead his or her protégé in terms of character formation, personal transformation and professional development.

Chapter Five, LISTENING asserts the incredible symphonic power of hearing and perceiving the thoughts, ideas and underlying motivations of the mentee.

Chapter Six, LEARNING develops the idea that the mentor relationship is an intricate tango of educational interaction that flows back and forth between the mentor and his or her protégé.

Chapter Seven, LAUGHING displays the powerful ability of humor to infuse the mentoring relationship with diverse moments that can help the mentee through even the toughest of life's circumstances.

Chapter Eight, LOVING embraces the essential need for unconditional positive regard. Unconditional positive regard is the integral fabric that sustains all effective mentoring relationships.

Let's continue our masterpiece!

CHAPTER FOUR

LEADING

The most powerful and effective tool in the mentor's arsenal is his/her ability to lead by example. Effective mentors strategically lead the mentee in character formation, personal transformation, and professional development.

"A good example has twice the value of good advice."
- Albert Schweitzer

"Children have never been very good at listening to their elders, but they have never failed to imitate them."
- James Baldwin

"I always try to teach by example, and not force my ideas on a young musician. One of the reasons we're here is to be a part of this process of exchange."
- Dizzy Gillespie

"Tell me and I forget, teach me and I may remember, involve me and I learn."
- Benjamin Franklin

Smiling From Ear to Ear

8:30am, Monday morning, Rena sat down at her desk and did a quick cursory glance at her burgeoning inbox. Excitedly, she noticed an email from her mentor, Alexandra. She loved receiving emails from Alexandra, especially on Monday mornings. Invariably, after reading Alexandra's missives (messages), her mornings always seem more focused, and her day is quantifiably more productive.

The email, sent at 4:45 that morning, was a short one:

"Good Morning Rena. I want you to know that I am really encouraged by the great progress you are making toward this month's goals. Keep up the great work! Also, I just sent you a calendar invite. If you are available, I would love for you to attend my biweekly team meeting next Monday. I have invited a guest speaker named Kevin Brown, who will be facilitating a workshop on personal and professional development. Not only is he an incredible motivator, but he also has an uncanny knack for identifying his clients' gifts and specific skill sets."

As she was reading, Rena realized, for just a moment that she was smiling from ear to ear. She was so grateful to have Alexandra in her corner. Her encouragement and timely wisdom had proven invaluable over the first few months of her career at Strategion. More importantly, Rena felt as if she finally had a blueprint for her professional and personal advancement. Not that she wanted to jump ship, but she sincerely believed that Alexandra was providing an excellent role model for her career development and progression. Earlier in her career, Rena had felt as if she was living a reactionary existence, and that all of her career decisions had been fueled by chance meetings, reactions and uncontrollable circumstances. Now, Rena finally imagined herself as the captain of her journey in that she felt as if she had the tools to successfully charter and navigate her course. The corresponding increase in Rena's confidence was exponential.

Alexandra's email continued,
"I have invited Kevin to lunch afterwards, and I was hoping that you could squeeze that in as well. Touch base with Freddie and let me know by Wednesday. Have a great week!"

Rena hit reply and began typing,
"Thanks Alexandra. I would love to sit in on the team meeting, and the guest speaker sounds really interesting. I will confirm everything with Freddie and let you know. Have a great day as well!"

Rena was excited about another opportunity to watch Alexandra in action. She had heard about Alexandra's team meetings and how they were challenging, productive, uplifting, and refreshing all at the same time.

That afternoon, Rena received the OK from Freddie, her team leader, and decided to give Alexandra a call instead of the usual email. "Good Afternoon, Alexandra. I know you're busy, but I wanted to call and let you know that I am good to go for your biweekly team meeting next week."

"That is great!" Alexandra was inwardly thankful to hear a friendly voice.

Rena continued, "Freddie also encouraged me to go to lunch with you and Kevin Brown. He said that Kevin was an amazing speaker and an incredible person. Thanks again! Are you doing OK today?"

"I'm good, Rena. Thanks for the call!" Alexandra was having a particularly challenging day, so she was happy to receive a call from her protégé. Her interactions with Rena always seemed to remind her to keep things in perspective. Alexandra continued, "I look forward to seeing you next week. Also, don't forget to send me an update on your goals. I am very interested in hearing your thoughts about the progress you are making."

A Different Kind of Team Meeting

The following week, Alexandra opened the biweekly team meeting in her usual encouraging manner. And, in keeping with her usual custom, she asked her trademark leading question, "Can someone begin our meeting by identifying and sharing one positive development since our last meeting?"

In an instant, Rena reflected back to the team meeting that she had attended on her first day of work. Immediately, she noticed a considerable difference: **Alexandra's team's energy was incredible. The attendees were positive, engaged, and enthusiastic.** Mesmerized, Rena soaked it all in.

The team meeting concluded with a 30-minute presentation by Kevin Brown, who was engaging, challenging and inspiring. In addition, he encouraged Alexandra's team to be "H.E.R.O.s," and, further, encouraged them to re-evaluate their own personal and professional goals vis-a-vis Strategion's corporate goals to **determine if there was any synergistic energy that could be tapped.** Kevin had a way of re-igniting enthusiasm in people by reminding them of **their inherent talents and potential.**

Once again, Rena could not help but analyze the differences between her marketing team meetings and Alexandra's finance team's meetings. Alexandra had set the tone at the outset of the meeting, and had encouraged contributions across the board. In addition to her words of encouragement, she also had made it a point to healthily challenge her team members in areas of deficiency, or in situations in which expectations had not been met. **Alexandra modeled leadership on many different levels**, and Rena felt so privileged to have witnessed it first-hand, and therein to have learned important skills that she knew would help her many times in the future.

Lunch with The Mentor's Mentor

Although Alexandra had focused all of her attention on Rena, she was equally excited about lunch with Kevin. She had met Kevin about five years ago, and had made it a point to periodically check in with him for professional accountability and to bounce ideas off of. His positive energy and enthusiasm were infectious. For the sake of time, Alexandra ordered carryout, and the three of them hunkered down in the Strategion boardroom.

Skipping formalities, Kevin cut to the chase and asked Rena about her new job and her mentoring relationship with Alexandra. Then, the conversation shifted to discuss Alexandra's niche in the company, her skill set, and the trajectory of her career. Thirty minutes went by quickly, and Alexandra and Kevin left for the airport.

As Rena headed back to her office, she mused to herself that it had been a very full and productive morning, especially watching Alexandra; she had gained invaluable insight about how to lead and motivate a team. Rena had also taken note of Alexandra's collegial interaction with Kevin.

On the way to the airport, Alexandra was sure to maximize every minute of time that she had with Kevin.

"Kevin, thanks again for taking the time to help motivate my staff. Also, the time with Rena was stellar. I want Rena to be surrounded by mentors and peers who are motivated by the pursuit of personal and professional excellence. When you have a moment, please take a few seconds to look over our company's mentoring framework. I just sent them to you in a PDF, but it will only take a couple of minutes to give you a good overview."

"It's great that your company has recognized the powerful value of mentoring its team members." Kevin leaned in.

Alexandra said, "Ok, here are the five areas that Strategion's Mentoring Program encourages its mentors to focus on. We learned about them in our mentor training sessions, and affectionately call them "the Five C's of Performance and Personal Life:

Core,

Craft,

Career,

Community, and

Compartments

As their car was nearing the airport, Kevin replied, "Alexandra, these are incredible! I will look over the PDF and provide my recommendations, but I will leave you with one point of advice. Make sure that you lead Rena by example in all five areas. **I have found that my most effective mentoring is caught, not taught.** You must lead by example, and remember – she is watching you like a hawk! But in a good way!"

Alexandra pulled into the departing flights lane, saying, "Thanks again, Kevin. You are a pretty good mentor yourself!"

Kevin rolled his eyes, smiled, grabbed his bag, and began to step out of the car, saying, "My pleasure, Alexandra. Don't forget that our next benchmark meeting is scheduled for the end of this month. I will be excited to hear about the progress you will have made by then toward your goals!"

Mentoring Your Mentee's CORE

CORE beliefs are basic beliefs about oneself and other people, as well as the world in which they live. These beliefs are things that they hold to be absolute truths deep down, underneath all their "surface" thoughts. **Essentially, core beliefs determine how one perceives and interprets the world.** They sit in the basement of one's mind. When something happens, their mind opens the basement, and consults the core belief(s) that is (are) most likely to keep them safe, and defend them against the world.

CORE beliefs are very important to a protégé because those beliefs determine to what degree he/she sees himself/herself as worthy, safe, competent, powerful, and loved.

Negative self-beliefs espoused by a mentor's protégé are deadly to his/her self-acceptance and self-esteem. **The protégé's core beliefs have a huge influence on their sense of belonging, as well as on the basic picture of how they feel they are viewed and treated by others.**

Not that a mentor needs to be a psychiatrist or psychoanalyst, but having a general understanding of one's mentee's CORE provides a clearer picture of how to motivate and inspire them to excel, achieve, and actualize their highest potential. This is extremely beneficial when in the course of a mentoring relationship, the protégé experiences the inevitable failures and setbacks. For example, understanding a mentee's CORE provides context with which to understand destructive patterns of thought and behavior that are necessary to charter new paths and new plans.

To gain the valuable insight and understanding of a mentee's CORE, employers and mentoring companies often employ the use of personality assessments, performance evaluations, and interpersonal communication skills inventories. These assessment tools, when coupled with frank and honest conversations, can provide a great deal of information, insight, and perspective that will assist and fuel the entire mentoring engagement.

Alexandra was excited to get her copy of Rena's DISC assessment, and, although she knew that the findings would not be one hundred percent accurate, she knew that the results would provide her with a great deal of relevant information about Rena's personality traits and dispositions. The DISC assessment tool is essentially nonjudgmental in that it does not place value on, or elevate, certain personality traits over others. Consequently, it has the potential to fuel the conversation about the mentee's CORE strengths and weaknesses in addition to:

- How a mentee usually responds to conflict, and how they solve problems

- What motivates them, and/or what things tend to stress them out
- How well they likely would work strategically as a team member
- Patterns of conflict avoidance that they might tend to have
- What strategies likely would work best to improve their interpersonal communication skills
- What would likely work best to increase their work performance and their customer service skills, especially relative to varying customer personality types.

Such knowledge would be key to finding Rena's inherent leadership style, CORE motivations, and incentives for success, thereby resulting in increased productivity and increased output.

Mentoring a Mentee's CRAFT

It goes without saying that the beautiful art of mastery does not solely apply to renowned musicians, or famous athletes. Mastering one's CRAFT applies to every discipline imaginable. In fact, the mere reality that each individual is as unique as the human thumbprint, while simultaneously being an unprecedented amalgamation of nature and nurture, provides us with the impetus to believe that **an individual's CRAFTS can never be duplicated or replicated!** That is, we are incredibly and inexplicably unrivaled! So **varied are individuals' CRAFTS that each mentee can be powerfully encouraged by their mentor to pursue their unique contribution to the world with sheer reckless abandon!** Love It!!!! This is the heart of your book!!!!!

It should also be noted that the meaning of the word CRAFT has a Germanic origin, and connotes an individual's "power, physical strength, or might." Over time, the Old English began to expand the meaning to include an individual's mental power that could be utilized to produce a certain "skill, dexterity, art, science, or talent." What an appropriate definition! For the sake of our discussion here, **a mentee's CRAFT can effectively be defined as the mentee's unique and essential proficiencies, talents, and giftings.**

On a practical level, a mentor can highlight, champion, and provide much needed motivation for their mentees' professional development. For example, if a mentee's "CRAFT" is corporate finance, public speaking, or graphic design, their mentor can recommend specific classes, courses, and educational material to make the mentee the best in their field. A mentor also holds the tremendous opportunity to **provide seasoned words of encouragement and affirmation at just the right time.**

Mentoring Your Mentee's CAREER

According to a recent survey from the American Society for Training and Development, "Seventy-five percent of executives say that mentoring has been critical to their CAREER development," and that "these relationships are invaluable in helping to make important professional decisions." The mentor's role in a mentee's CAREER development should never be minimized, and such mentoring can effectively occur at the beginning, middle, and even at the end of one's professional journey. The mentoring process provides support for the mentee's CAREER planning that includes:

- Unbiased feedback with regard to the strengths and weaknesses of their mentee. This can prove especially valuable when the mentee is unable to talk freely with their supervisor.
- Objective evaluation of the mentee's performance and passions, and how each would potentially affect the career trajectory of the mentee.
- Available career paths, combined with knowledge of various organizational hierarchies that could be recognized by a seasoned mentor, but totally hidden from the consciousness of younger professionals.
- The ability of the mentee to connect and network with other individuals in their chosen field.

The effects of mentor influence could be seen in the lives of Shawn and Anderson, as well as Alexandra and Rena. Although a mentor should never assume the captain's role in the steering of their protégé's career-ship, a mentor can provide helpful hints, tools, life hacks, and advice as their protégé navigates the waters of their chosen CAREER path.

These mentor distinctions and capabilities are also applicable to, and important for, the mentor who mentors a young person who is early in their selected career. Explaining potential CAREER paths, and their academic requirements, vocational programs, public service roles, and humanitarian efforts are important topics that should be discussed with a young person who is attempting to find their place in the world. **A seasoned mentor can be a powerful ally who understands how a mentee's unique, particular CORE will help direct and sustain their desired CAREER path.**

Mentoring a Mentee's COMMUNITY

Mentor Joe had prepared Isaiah, instructing him to wear some old jeans and a sweatshirt. Arriving at Isaiah's house early Saturday morning, Joe handed him a warm bagel and a bottle of freshly-squeezed orange juice. "Good morning, Isaiah! My team and I are participating in the Anacostia River clean-up, and they are excited to have you join us. We participate twice a year, as a way to give back to our community, develop relationships, and just have fun outside of the office."

Gerrod A.M. Williamson, Community Programs Specialist for the Johns Hopkins University Center for Social Concern defines COMMUNITY as, "who or what an individual chooses to align themselves with, how an individual chooses to engage with people of similar or differing identities, and how an individual chooses to interact with the person to their right and to their left. **COMMUNITY is the essence of who we are as social beings.**"

COMMUNITY is a social organization or unit that shares a common thread. **Whether norms, religion, values, geographic proximity, political ideologies, values, customs, or the many classifications of identity, these characteristics unite people resulting in a COMMUNITY."**

Well-known motivational speaker, Tony Robbins, says, "**The secret to living is giving!**" Mentoring in the corporate arena as well as in youth-based mentoring organizations, provide many multifaceted opportunities for the personal and professional growth of the mentee. Consequently, **when a mentor models the importance of COMMUNITY engagement and involvement, it allows the mentee to experience, first-hand, the holistic benefits of embracing a philanthropic worldview.** Here are a few benefits of modeling COMMUNITY engagement with a mentee:

- **It gives a mentee a sense of purpose.** Futility is one of the biggest reasons why many people feel unfulfilled. Giving back to the COMMUNITY, however, gives a mentee a greater sense of purpose. They will wake up each day, knowing that they are about to do something meaningful for their COMMUNITY by effecting positive change and helping to transform lives.
- **It is good for a mentee's health.** Studies have shown that those who spend more time volunteering in their COMMUNITY develop a greater sense of purpose in life, thereby entirely changing their outlook on life. For example, they are much more motivated to live healthier lifestyles in order to achieve their goals: they sleep better, eat better, and have well-managed schedules.
- **It widens a mentee's network.** Widening a mentee's network means creating more opportunities for the future. **Being connected with people and organizations in their COMMUNITY puts the mentee in a better position to take his/her career further.**
- **It teaches a mentee to look outward.** When a mentee is so caught up with personal problems, they tend to overlook other factors, such as the COMMUNITY in which they live, and the area that they inhabit.
- **It unlocks a mentee's potential skills.** A lot of volunteers discover their greatest skills (CRAFT) while on the "mission field." Whether one is giving back to a local or international COMMUNITY, volunteering helps a mentee to discover and hone their skills.
- **It shares a mentee's expertise.** Another benefit of a mentee giving back to their COMMUNITY is that it shares their expertise. Whether she/he is good in construction, music, or mathematics, sharing her/his talent with the world can give hope and change many lives – sometimes in amazing, unexpected ways!

- **It boosts a mentee's self-esteem.** One more benefit of giving back to one's COMMUNITY is that it boosts a mentee's self-esteem. **There is nothing more self-affirming than knowing that you are doing something good, and making a difference!**

Leading Your Mentee's COMPARTMENTS

Unable to focus, the bags under Rena's eyes had become so pronounced that Alexandra knew that it was time to intervene. "Wow! You look really run down. What is going on with you?"

Alexandra would never have spoken to one of her colleagues in such a direct manner; however, because of the relationship that she had established with her mentee, she sensed that a more direct approach was necessary.

In the middle of their conversation, Alexandra leaned in a little and continued, "You have been really tired lately, and I have noticed that you seem to be having a difficult time concentrating."

Rena immediately jumped on the defensive, "What are you talking about? I'm fine!"
Alexandra did not blink; she was not fazed or put off by her mentee's response. As a matter of fact, she expected it. However, she knew that she would have to gather more substantive data to convince Rena that her life was a little out of balance.

Five signs that you might be a workaholic:
- You work longer than your colleagues,
- You can't turn off,
- Your body feels unwell,
- Your relationships are strained, and
- You tie your self-worth to your work success.
"Here, look at this quote from Steven Covey."

Alexandra handed the small plaque on her desk to Rena. "Read it to me."

Rena grabbed it and read it slowly and pensively to herself; then she spoke the words out loud.

> **"The key is not to prioritize what's on your schedule,**
> **but to schedule your priorities."**

Rena's eyes began to well up, and she quickly glanced away in order to hide her emotions from Alexandra.

"I need to run to the restroom quickly. I will be right back." Rena quickly set her laptop down and rushed out of Alexandra's office.

About ten minutes passed before she returned and plopped down into the big brown leather chair across from Alexandra's bookshelf.

"How much more time do you have before your next appointment?" Rena started slowly. Alexandra was glad that Rena had returned and was willing to process. She had noticed the stress in Rena's eyes, and had been concerned about Rena's performance on the job. "No worries. I've got a team huddle in about an hour."

As soon as Alexandra closed the office door, Rena broke down, "Alexandra, my parents are getting a divorce. I know that this happens to half of the population, but my parents have been married for twenty-seven years. Not only that, but they are also trying to pull me into the middle of it by trying to make me choose sides. I have not gotten any sleep in the last three weeks, and it has been an absolute nightmare!"

Alexandra sat down in the chair next to Rena. "Rena, this is no small matter. I know that your job means a lot to you, and that you are trying to meet your performance goals, but your family and your mental health should always be your number one priority. I am going to recommend that you take advantage of our family leave policy in order to sort through things with your parents. I am not telling you what to do, but I am telling you what to do."

Rena nodded as Alexandra continued, "I heard an awesome talk from Brian Dyson who used to be the Vice Chairman and COO at Coca-Cola. He said, "Imagine life as a game in which you are juggling five balls in the air. You name them – work, family, health, friends, and spirit, and you're keeping all of these in the air at the same time. **You will soon understand that work is a rubber ball. If you drop it, it will bounce back. But the other four balls are made of glass. If you drop one of these, they will be irrevocably scuffed, marked, nicked, damaged, or even shattered. Then, they will never be the same.** You must understand that, and strive for balance in your life."

As a mentor, it is also very important to model an equitable work-life balance in front of your protégé. Being able to clearly prioritize family, work, health, friends and fun are critical to a protégé's professional and personal success.

Brushstrokes

An essential element in The Art of Effective Mentoring is leading your mentee in these five areas – CORE, CRAFT, CAREER, COMMUNITY, and COMPARTMENTS. And it "goes without saying" that **the mentor always leads by example. That way, the mentee can be exposed to, and thereby learn the methods, procedures, values, and culture of the organization by observing the mentor's behavior.** However, bad habits can also be inherited by the mentee, so it is paramount that mentors are aware of their own conduct, and what it is that they are imparting.

The mentor should take time to bring the mentee to meetings that are above their usual level in order to understand the bigger picture of the organization. This also can inspire the mentee to pursue future opportunities at a higher level. The mentor should also take time to review these meetings and opportunities with the mentee to share their perspectives, and to ask for the mentee's thoughts on what they have observed.

Randi Frank writes, "One of my mentees had the opportunity to watch me conduct job interviews that are usually private. Afterwards, we took time to discuss each interview, including remarks from my mentee's notes on the interviews. It provided the mentee an opportunity that, normally, she would not have had, in a safe environment, and it also gave me a second perspective on each of the interviews. In addition, it gave my mentee an opportunity to see the interview from the interviewer's perspective, which, undoubtedly, will benefit her at her next job interview – whenever that may occur!"

CHAPTER FIVE

LISTENING

It cannot be understated that listening is the critical underpinning that supports and upholds every successful mentoring engagement

"Most people do not listen with the intent to understand; they listen with the intent to reply."
- Stephen R. Covey

"Courage is what it takes to stand up and speak. Courage is also what it takes to sit down and listen."
- Winston Churchill

"My personal experience leads me to believe that, fundamentally, communication skills, and specifically listening skills, are at the root of what makes someone a great and effective mentor."
- Jeanne-Marie Daly

A Quick Word to the Reader

Dear Mentor or Program Director, I sincerely believe that one's effectiveness as a mentor is directly proportional to his or her ability to listen. If the mentor is not able to effectively read between the lines and listen between the phrases, they will be largely ineffective in their attempt to connect with the CORE and underlying life motivations of the mentee. If the mentee does not feel that, or if she/he has not been heard or understood, there will, eventually over time, be an unfortunate breakdown in the vital connection that MUST exist for a mentor-mentee relationship to move beyond transactional interactions to transformational exchanges.

Too Much Coffee?

Mentor Joe and Mentee Isaiah sat at the high-top table in the café. Suddenly, their conversation had come to a screeching halt, and the tension that was in the air could be cut with a knife. Joe realized that his "come-to-Jesus" meeting with his mentee was not progressing as he had initially planned. Isaiah was visibly frustrated, and was passive aggressively falling back into his habit of apathetic silence.

The whole situation began with a call from Ms. Minor. In complete exasperation she, explained to Joe her sore displeasure with regard to Mentee Isaiah's recent academic performance. Coming out of the rather one-sided discussion with Isaiah, Joe concluded that he would have to schedule the aforementioned "come-to-Jesus" meeting with Isaiah in order to explain the life-ruining ramifications of poor grades.

Note: *Often a mentor can bring, with good intentions, their own agenda with presumptions and presuppositions to specific conversations, and to the mentoring relationship as a whole. In doing so, it can prevent the mentee from writing their own script, owning their own story, and fulfilling their unique purpose – apart from outside influence and external manipulation. Consequently, the mentor should regularly take a step back to assess if their posture is controlling or collaborating.*

More Talking Versus Mindful Listening

Maybe it was too much coffee that morning, but when Joe became fully aware that he had been talking non-stop, he paused for a moment, grounded himself, and took time to breathe. He then redirected his thoughts, and made a calculated decision to focus and pay closer attention to what Isaiah had to say. He remembered the powerful concept of "mindful listening," and quickly decided that this was the opportune time to practice what he had learned. "Hey, I'm sorry, Isaiah. I just realized that I have been doing most of the talking. Why don't you tell me, what's going on? I really need to hear your side of the story."

Oddly enough, Joe had learned how to practice mindful listening from one of his own personal mentors, Jon Kabat-Zinn. Recalling one of Jon Kabat-Zinn's sessions, Joe remembered that being present in the moment, and really hearing what your mentee is saying, is a crucial step toward developing trust in a mentoring relationship, or in any relationship for that matter. The intentional building of trust subsequently facilitates a greater exchange and flow of ideas. Isaiah looked at Joe, unsure how best to proceed. Unfortunately, Isaiah had grown accustomed to being chastised for sharing his feelings, thoughts, and ideas. He looked like a deer in the headlights as he quickly tried to assess whether he was in a safe space.

Joe could sense that Isaiah harbored some trepidation, and urged him on, "Really Isaiah, you can tell me what's going on at school, and with your grades. I want you to know that you are in a safe space. I know how intelligent you are, but I can look at your expressions and tell that something is bothering you. "What is it?" Joe paused, figuratively stepped back, and gave Isaiah the space to respond without pressure.

Isaiah breathed out a sigh of apparent discomfort, but pressed into the moment; over their time together, he had grown to trust Mr. Joe to a certain extent, and, for Joe, this would be another one of the tests of their relationship. Isaiah had been burned before by relatives, teachers, and even friends that he had confided in, and he did not want to get burned again.

 "Mr. Joe, my football coach told me that if I worked a little harder, I would have a strong chance to be the starting running back next year. So, I have been spending extra time at practice after school, and less time at home. When I get home, I am tired and worn out, so I don't have time to finish my homework."

Isaiah paused for a second, continuing to test the waters. Joe nodded, opened his posture, and leaned in. "I am listening."

Isaiah took a breath and continued, "My grades suck. I had two exams last week that I barely studied for because I kept falling asleep in my books. My mom is never home since she picked up an extra shift at the hospital. I hate math, I'm not good at it - and when I have questions about my homework, there is nobody to ask for help. My mom expects me to do well, but I don't know how. On top of that she's never around when I need her. When she is home, she is too tired."

Joe was so thankful that he had taken a moment to step back and practice mindful listening. It became blatantly obvious that Isaiah did not need another "come-to-Jesus meeting." Rather, Isaiah needed someone to listen and empathically understand his situation.

Principles of Mindful Listening

In "Get Out of Your Head: Mindful Listening for Project Managers," author Charlie Scott describes 3 key principles to mindful listening:

Principle 1 = CURRENT
Mindful listening requires being fully present in the moment, and paying full attention to the person to whom you are listening, and without distraction.

Principle 2 = CULTIVATE
Cultivate empathy requires seeing things from the perspective of the mentee,

making eye contact, mimicking facial expressions, and acknowledging the mentee's views and validating their authenticity.

Principle 3 = CUES

Listening to your own cues requires the listener to pay attention to how their body and thoughts are responding during a conversation. This process also requires the listener to be aware of their own inherent biases that may cloud how they react to or respond to the other person.

Yet another principle of mindful listening is **CULTIVATING EMPATHY.** Empathic listening involves listening to your mentee attentively, without interrupting, and responding by restating, in your own words, what you think they said and what you understand their feelings to be. Furthermore, when interpreting your mentee's feelings, be sensitive to the emotions being expressed, and do your best to understand the situation from their point of view based on their own experience or worldview. Your response should be non-judgmental, and you should refrain from interjecting your own feelings or opinions – even if you disagree with what they are saying.

No Interruptions Please!

Resist the strong urge to interject your feelings, opinions or experiences this would give the impression that you, the mentor, are more concerned with expressing your views than listening to the mentee.

A mentor's interjections and interruptions invariably short-circuit the mentee's willingness to share in the present, and, further, would sabotage any future potential discussions. Remember: This is about your mentee, not about you!

After listening carefully to Isaiah's response, Joe commended him for being honest and transparent, "Wow! It sounds like you are in an extremely tough place. I'm hearing you say that you could use some extra help studying math.

Would it be helpful if I talked with your Mom about getting a math tutor?" asked Joe.

"I don't know - maybe. But we don't have the money for private lessons, and I'd honestly rather be playing football," Isaiah replied.

"I understand; but if we can't get your grade up to a C or better, your coach won't let you play anyway. The library offers free tutoring on Tuesdays and Thursdays after school. I have a friend who volunteers there that I'd like you to meet. Let's take a look at your practice schedule and see what we can fit in. If I set this up, would you be willing to go?"

"Do I have a choice?" Isaiah seemed reluctant.

"You always have a choice, Isaiah. And right now, you have the choice to try something different, like tutoring, and see if it helps improve your confidence and your grades, or you can keep doing the same thing and be in danger of failing math this semester and jeopardizing your football career. If you make the choice to invest in yourself by studying, I think you, your Mom, and your coach will all see improvement in your math grades. Besides, I think you might enjoy meeting my friend, Dakari."

Stepping back from the conversation and really listening, allowed Joe to see things from Isaiah's perspective, and allowed him to cultivate empathy for Isaiah as well, and take a different approach from harshly criticizing or trying to force him into tutoring. Joe knew it had to be Isaiah's decision, or he wouldn't put forth the effort involved to be successful. He also knew that, if he could get Isaiah to a tutoring session with Dakari, who also happened to have a degree in Sports Medicine, he might expand Isaiah's horizons a bit more.

Finally, by being present in the moment during the conversation with Isaiah, Joe was able to "listen to his own cues" – the third principle of mindful listening. **"Listening to your own cues"** takes practice. It is the ability to tune into how your body and mind are reacting when listening to your mentee.

This includes noticing how their words might make you feel, without acting on those feelings. Of the three principles of mindful listening, being able to "listen to your own cues" probably takes the most work, because it requires the listener to be willing to explore their own inherent biases in how they see and interpret the world around them. It also prompts the mentor to understand that his or her sense of "reality" may be very different from their mentee's. This is especially important in building trust and removing judgment in a mentoring relationship.

Joe listened to his own cues and recognized his own disappointment with Isaiah's lack of improvement in his grades. Instead of reacting or judging, "the pause" in the conversation allowed Joe to give Isaiah the space he needed to speak his mind, and to not only be heard by Joe, but to feel like he was being listened to by his mentor.

According to American author David Augsburger, "Being heard is so close to being loved that, for the average person, they are almost indistinguishable." Fortunately, Joe had slowly been building trust with Isaiah during the course of their mentorship, and once he took the time to slow down and listen, Isaiah started to reveal what was really going on.

"Okay, let's go back to the goals you set for yourself when we met a few months ago, and together, we'll figure out where we go from here."

When they looked at Isaiah's goals – they found that he was actually excelling at his physical goals, which helped boost his confidence. His coach had also made him team captain – not only because of his talent on the field, but also because he worked well with other members of the team, and demonstrated strong leadership skills.

At the end of the session, Joe and Isaiah set forth a plan for better time management with his schoolwork. Then, Joe signed Isaiah up for tutoring sessions with Dakari twice a week at the library. They would spend 30 minutes after school before football practice working on his math. Also, the month before finals, they met up for an extra hour each week to study.

A week later, Joe called Isaiah to see how the tutoring sessions were going.

"Okay." Isaiah replied. "Dakari is pretty cool. He told me he had to study math to become a physical therapist, and he works with the Baltimore Ravens! He said if I pass math with a B or better, he'll invite me and my mom out to a game! I'm thinking that, if I can get a scholarship, I might want to study Sports medicine while I pursue football."

Brushstrokes

In closing, **it cannot be understated that listening is the critical underpinning that supports and upholds every successful mentoring**

engagement. It "goes without saying" that there are many powerful benefits that occur when a mentor chooses to embrace the discipline of listening. Here are a few of them:

1. Listening Facilitates Solidarity Listening is critical to every relationship, and the mentoring relationship is no exception. Without effective listening, trust cannot be established. Effective listening enables and empowers the mentor to connect with his/her mentee at a deeper level. From this deeper level, the mentor can tap into the CORE of the mentee. Very often, mentees put walls up and become stoic and reserved if they feel that the mentor is not listening, or seeking to push his agenda at the expense of the mentee's desires. Consequently, **if the mentee feels that the mentor has become another pushy, overbearing parent, the mentoring relationship will be relegated to a dictatorial, one-sided exchange of ideas.**

2. Listening Facilitates Solutions
If Joe had not taken the time to listen to Isaiah, not only would he have missed an opportunity to connect with his mentee, but also Joe might have

missed the opportunity to help Isaiah find an expedient solution to his problem. **Without listening intently to Isaiah's subtle cues, Joseph or Joe would have overlooked the deeper issues that were sabotaging his scholastic performance.** Fortunately, because Joe took a moment to abandon his own agenda and preconceived notions/biases, he was able to listen intently, and clearly assess the underlying factors that were affecting Isaiah's academic success.

3. Listening Facilitates Self-Esteem
In the mentoring relationship, nothing validates the mentee more than the realization that he/she is being heard, and that his/her thoughts and opinions are important. Glenn R. Schiraldi, Ph.D., author of The Self Esteem Workbook, describes **healthy self-esteem as a realistic, appreciative opinion of oneself.** A mentor that listens can only serve to strengthen his mentee's esteem

4. Listening Facilitates Sacred Space
Have you ever walked into a large cathedral, or a museum filled with priceless artifacts? These are sacred spaces that command an attitude of reverence, awe and respect. Similarly, when a mentee shares a sensitive moment or an emotional event from her personal story, she is allowing her mentor into a sacred space that presupposes great caution and care. It is precisely at these listening moments that the mentor must figuratively take off their shoes to acknowledge the incredible privilege of being allowed to walk on the holy ground of another human's heart.

CHAPTER SIX

LEARNING

Mentoring relationships are never a unilateral transaction. The mentor must be receptive to embrace the inevitability that the mentee will also provide many learning opportunities as a result of the mentor-mentee relationship

You should never try to be better than someone else, you should always be learning from others. But you should never cease trying to be the best you could be because that's under your control and the other isn't.
- John Wooden, UCLA Basketball Coach Hall of Fame

A great teacher is someone who can learn from their students, who can learn with them, and who learns for them.
- Robert John Meehan, Educator

"My students encouraged me to have no fear. They're resilient – they have to be. I don't like heights, but they inspired me to jump off a jetty during an Outward Bound course in Wales. If they can throw themselves at life's challenges, then so can I."
- Aaron Ramsbottom, Language Instructor

Learning from Your Mentee

An aspect of effective mentorship that often goes unnoticed is the acknowledgement of the many traits, talents, experiences, and expertise that a mentee brings to the table. **This oversight frequently takes place in hierarchical environments that elevate the mentor to a non-human superior status, while relegating the mentee to a position of inferiority. This patriarchal mindset can often produce negative and restricting implications for the mentoring exchange.** On the other hand, when the mentor is able to view herself/himself as a facilitator of knowledge, rather than a repository, the result is a collaborative, healthy exchange of ideas between mentor and mentee. The result, over the course of the mentoring engagement, is that the mentor will frequently find himself/herself being "mentored" by the mentee.

If you are thinking of mentoring someone, here are a few things that you can expect to learn from them.

1.   Learning Generational Nuances

Depending on the age difference between a mentor and their mentee, there is a good chance that a generational gap exists. Spending time with a young, professional mentee can give the mentor a better understanding of what other generations — for example, Millennials — want with their careers, and how they expect to be managed. The more that a mentor interacts with professional mentees of all ages, the better they will understand their mentee's wants, needs, CORE and COMMUNITY and needs.

Sometimes, issues that arise in a mentor's office, while mentoring, can be attributed to simple generational differences. Conflict management, communication, and engagement techniques can vary between generations. And, although a mentor may feel that they handle such issues well, spending time with a mentee from a different generation may be exactly what the mentor may need to become a better leader.

2.   Learning Leadership Skills

Regardless of a mentor's career level, they can always use more leadership training; and developing a new relationship with a mentee may do just that. When a mentee looks to a mentor for guidance, it makes the mentor more aware of what they themselves are communicating in word and action. This self-awareness is a great skill to hone when leading others, and can be further developed while serving as a mentor.

From the start of a new mentor-mentee relationship, it is vitally important for the mentor to establish open communication between their self and their mentee. The mentor should inform the new mentee to be honest about how they perceive their joint mentee-mentor interaction, and learn from that interaction. Sometimes it is hard to see one's own faults as a leader; so, having a mentee point out areas needing improvement can help the mentor lead others more effectively.

3.   Learning Updated Techniques and Technology

Chances are that a mentee will be closer to college or grad school than their mentor is. In every industry, procedures change, and techniques get updated. When a mentor has a mentoring relationship with a high-schooler, or with someone who just graduated from college, or with someone who just completed professional training, this can actually help a mentor stay current in their field.

Before giving advice, a mentor should make it a constant practice to ask their mentee how they (the mentee) would approach a situation, or handle a particular problem, then analyze the mentee's thought processes. Just because a mentor has more experience in a particular field than their mentee, does not mean that the mentor cannot learn something from their mentee. For example, if the mentor is a seasoned executive, they may feel face-to-face is the most effective way of communicating with their mentees; however, younger generations may feel completely comfortable, for example, connecting with people online. **When a mentor better understands technological advances and how some people do business differently, then this sets the stage, in being able to more effectively and more efficiently interact with others, including with their mentees.**

Mentorships are a great way for a mentor to impart knowledge to other professionals, but they are also a great way for a mentor to learn how to be a better leader themself. **A good mentor will always be ready to learn – including being surprised at what a mentee can teach them!**

Mentee Shawn

It was 5:00 on a Monday afternoon, and Shawn was ready to leave his office when his phone rang. He considered not answering it, but when he looked at the screen, he realized that it was Anderson Cruse. Exactly six months had passed since Shawn had bid him farewell in Tennessee. Shawn picked up the phone, "Anderson Cruse?" "Hey, Shawn! I'm so glad you answered. I was afraid that you might be gone for the day." Anderson sounded relieved and excited at the same time. "I was just discussing something with a coworker, and your name came up. I wanted to check-in with you and see if you had given my proposal any thought." Anderson paused before continuing, "And I admit that I have ulterior motives."

Shawn had thought about the mentorship, but he had also taken on more work at his job, and had not really had time to give Troy and Anderson's mentoring offer any further consideration. "What sort of ulterior motives?" asked Shawn.

The West Coast Connection

Anderson started in, "Well, at our first meeting, you talked about your goals for your career path, and I remember you mentioning that flexibility was important to you – the ability to work from anywhere so you that aren't tied to one place."

"Yes," agreed Shawn, still guarding his emotions.

"Well," Anderson proceeded cautiously, "...my company, Delta Strategies, has made the decision to expand into the global marketplace. We are looking for a global IT consultant who would eventually train and lead an international team of consultants. I thought of you immediately, and wondered if you'd be interested in reconnecting in Seattle and interviewing for the position. I know you have valuable expertise with mergers and acquisitions, and I think we could really use your perspectives and your experience...I think you'd be a great fit."

Shawn did not know what to say. "Uh. Wow. This is very sudden. Can you tell me more about the position?"

Anderson, "Of course. But I wanted to connect with you by phone first." Anderson paused. "Shawn, I know that our first mentorship attempt did not go so well, and I take full responsibility for that. I came to realize that, when I moved to Seattle, I did not handle that transition well. I was quite overwhelmed at the time and did an extremely poor job of communicating. Oddly enough, you had actually taught me how to improve my own leadership skills."

"When this present position came up, I thought it was so perfect for you. I will send you all the information about this position in an email. Look it over, and let me know what you think. Do you think you can get back with me before the end of the week?"
"Sure, Anderson, I should be able to do that." Shawn still did not know what to think.

"OK, great! Thanks Shawn. I really hope that you will consider this opportunity, and I prayerfully anticipate that it will give me an opportunity to provide restitution for my past sins!" Anderson chuckled, although he was quite serious. "I look forward to talking with you at the end of the week. Thanks, Shawn."

"Thanks, Anderson. Talk to you soon." Stunned, Shawn put his phone down on the desk and stared out the window.

Later that evening, Shawn checked his emails and found the job description for Delta Strategies' Global IT Consultant. The salary was significantly more than he was currently making, and with room to grow. He would be traveling back and forth to Seattle for meetings on occasion – but most of the work would be done remotely. There was also potential to travel and meet with new clients. Shawn decided he would at least throw his hat in the ring and interview for the position.

A week later, Shawn booked a flight to Seattle. Anderson met him at the Seattle airport.

"Shawn, thank you for coming out to interview with us. I think you really would be an asset to our company. Have you been to Seattle before?"

"No, this is my first time to the West Coast, Anderson, but I do hope to see more of it when I have time. Anderson, I appreciate that you thought of me for this opportunity. To be honest, after the way you left so abruptly way back when, I was having a very difficult time with self-doubt, and, to myself, I questioned your integrity."

"I'm sorry, Shawn. Not to make excuses, but things were moving so fast for me. I had such a short time to wrap up my life on the East Coast, and then move out here. Hear me, that's not an excuse for my behavior. I admit that I did not handle the situation well. I should have contacted you and offered to put the mentorship on hold until I sorted things out, or even asked Troy for help in finding you another mentor. I definitely learned from my mistakes."

Shawn nodded, remaining neutral and taking it all in.

Continuing, Shawn said, "We have a full day ahead. Let's drop your bags at your hotel, and then grab some coffee so that I can catch you up on the job, and prepare you for the interview. You'll be meeting with the CEO of Delta Strategies, the new East Coast Director, and the HR Director. If you are offered the position, Shawn, you will not be working directly with me, so if continuing the mentorship is something you would want, I really would welcome that opportunity – whether you get the job or not. I think there's a lot we can learn from each other quite honestly. I have certainly found that mentoring is never a one-way exchange."

Seattle's Best

Anderson drove them to his favorite coffee joint just outside the office building that his company owned. As they sat down to coffee, Anderson prepared Shawn for the interview.

"Shawn, let me give you a heads up. There are four other candidates. Two have already been interviewed, and there are two more interviewing later this week. I wanted to brief you ahead of time to give you the best possible chance of nailing the interview."

"Right now, Delta Strategies is about to launch a global initiative using artificial intelligence to investigate water systems around the world. We are opening a new office on the East Coast. If you are hired for the position, that would be your main hub. We need someone with skills in developing artificial intelligence, and I know that you studied AI as part of your master's degree. This is why I think you'd be a great fit. – You are up to speed on some of the latest AI technology. In fact, you probably know more about it than I do."
"I can help you navigate the waters of a global company and working remotely – with travel required on a pretty regular basis. I usually travel twice a month either across the country or internationally. Additionally, I told the CEO about our mentorship, and she wants to start a mentoring program in the future, and is looking to create some standard procedures before getting it

off the ground."

Establishing Trust, Again

After the interview, Anderson met Shawn and offered to take him to dinner at his favorite Thai restaurant. "So, how did the interview go?" he asked.

"I think it went well. They asked a lot of questions about my experience in developing AI, as well as my experience working with diverse clients. As you know, I did a year abroad in Hong Kong."

"No, really? I did not know that. We will come back to the interview, but could you tell me more about your experience in Hong Kong?" Anderson purposefully began asking open-ended questions to get Shawn to open up. He wanted to get a greater perspective on Shawn's motivations and leadership style.

"Ah, man, working in Hong Kong was definitely one of my most challenging engagements. Learning a new culture and language really pushed me to step out of my comfort zone, and develop a greater sense of self-awareness and emotional intelligence."

"Explain." Anderson wanted Shawn to go deeper.

Shawn took a deep breath and shifted in his seat, somewhat unaccustomed to a line of questioning that caused him to introspect. "Well, it was really uncomfortable for me to have to continually ask for help. In the past, I had always prided myself on my independence and my ability to figure things out on my own. In Hong Kong, even though I had the technical expertise to do the job, I really had to trust and rely on my teammates to convey plans and ideas – which often left me feeling quite apprehensive."

Anderson made it a point to maintain eye contact, and show Shawn that he was actively engaged and listening intently. Anderson also knew that Shawn was moving into a 'sacred space.' "That must have been really tough. Would you do anything differently next time?"

Shawn's combative body language began to ease as he sensed Anderson's genuine concern. "You know, looking back, I probably would have trusted my team more during the earlier stages of the project. I think my initial guarded responses and interactions caused us to lose valuable time at the beginning of our engagement."

"Hmmmm. That's really good stuff. As leaders, we often are oblivious to how our interactions directly affect the performance of our team. You really seem to have a great sense of self-awareness, which is a critical component of emotional intelligence. I know that we have only begun, but I really appreciate you taking a chance to open up to me. I hope that you get this position."

The Call to Continuing Mentorship

Two weeks later, Shawn got a call from Delta Strategies with a job offer he couldn't turn down. Anderson followed up with a congratulatory phone call.

"Welcome to Delta Strategies, Shawn!" I look forward to seeing you in Seattle from time to time. "Have you given any thought to continuing our mentorship?"

"Thanks Anderson, I appreciate you encouraging me to apply for this opportunity. It really is beyond anything I could have imagined. And yes, I would like to give the mentorship another go. I think that I'd like to learn everything I can to prepare me for this new experience."

"Great! Let's make an appointment to meet when you come out to Seattle for your new employee orientation. I will reach out to Troy Robbs, and we'll set some new ground rules for our mentoring engagement!"

When Shawn returned to Seattle a while later for orientation, he and Anderson developed a new mentorship agreement that would serve as a protocol for future mentoring relationships at Delta Strategies. Anderson reviewed Shawn's list of short-term, mid-range, and long-term goals, and encouraged Shawn to identify and pursue several "stretch goals." They decided on weekly check-in phone calls for the first two months, as Shawn settled into his new position, followed by a monthly Zoom check-in. Also, they would meet in person every three months when Shawn was in Seattle for the first year of his employment.

Both acknowledged that the demands of their jobs and the time difference from East to West Coast would create challenges, but Anderson promised to make the mentorship a priority and block the dates/times they had agreed upon on his calendar. If anything did come up, they would maintain open and honest communication.

After all, this was a one-year commitment. At the end of the year, they could meet and re-evaluate. If things went well, they would work together to develop the protocol for the company's new mentoring program.

Three months later, Shawn flew to Seattle for his company's quarterly financial meetings. Even though Shawn made several budget and financial presentations, as planned, Shawn and Anderson were able to meet several times over the course of the week.

Anderson, in his quest to be a better mentor, had identified several key areas in which he planned to devote his professional development attention. Anderson also had determined to model and challenge Shawn to do the same.

Meet Maya the Mentor

Maya was finishing her junior year at college. She was studying social work, and had been volunteering with the Boys and Girls Club for two years when an advisor inspired her to volunteer with the World Relief Organization, which pairs mentors with immigrant youth to help acclimate them to their new country. The mentor assists the mentee with language skills and navigating the challenges of acculturation. Maya hoped to improve her skills working with children from many different backgrounds. Her advisor had stressed the value and rewards of learning communication skills for a variety of different clients from different backgrounds, and that this would be a great way to challenge herself.

When Maya signed up with World Relief, she was happy to discover that the organization had a thorough orientation process – including tools for language learning, and how to mentor across cultures. Simply by signing up to mentor, Maya was already gaining new skills that would benefit her resume and the trajectory of her future career.

Sema the Mentee

The mentorship coordinator from World Relief, Cheryl Saylor, was excited to pair Maya with Sema Abadi. Sema was from Syria. She and her family arrived in the U.S. having escaped violent conflict overseas. Sema was just 16 years old when she arrived, with two years left of high school before she would graduate. Her primary challenge was adjusting to a new school, a new country, a new culture, and a new way of life.

It was Maya's first time mentoring someone from another country, and she was a bit apprehensive because she did not speak any Arabic. But the Director of World Relief recommended a beginner course online, which also gave a brief introduction to Arabic culture. Maya remembered how difficult high school had been for her because her parents had moved in the middle of her sophomore year, and she had had to start over and get used to a new school in a foreign country. Their shared experience of starting a new school in the middle of high school, gave Sema and Maya common ground from which to build a relationship as they explored their different cultures.

4.   Learning Common Interests[15]

From the beginning of their relationship, Maya and Sema established their mutual "values" as family, food and fun! And "fun" included listening to music. Sema shared music from her culture with Maya, and Maya introduced Sema to hip hop and reggae. Their meetings often involved food, sometimes prepared by Sema and her mother, and sometimes, Maya would take Sema to her favorite sushi restaurant in the city. Through food, family, and fun, Maya and Sema began to build a foundation of trust.

Sema's family was very close-knit. Sema had entered the U.S. with her parents, younger brother, and baby sister. They had one other relative living in the United States, but most of her family was back in Syria. Sema missed her cousins and friends. Maya's parents had divorced after she went to college. Her father traveled a lot, so she rarely saw him, but she remained close to her mother and grandmother, and had a large extended family of cousins. She knew how important family was, and also what it was like to miss those who were not present.

Maya and Sema had decided in their initial planning and goal-setting meetings (see the chapter on legislating), to meet once a week during the school year to help Sema improve her understanding of the English language. Sema had also set an aggressive goal to be able to study at her grade level by the end of the school year. Sema already spoke English pretty well, but needed some help with grammar and writing. The learning quickly became a two-way street – with Sema teaching Maya basic conversation skills in Arabic.

---

[15]This is a continuation of the Shawn and Anderson's Learning List

Whenever she met with Sema, Maya was always greeted by either her or her mother and was always invited in for tea and sweets. "As-salamu alaykum, Mrs. Abadi." Maya greeted Sema's Mom with the little bit of Arabic she had learned.

5.   Learning Each Other's Language

"Wa 'alaikum salaam, Maya. Please come in." replied Mrs. Abadi. "Sema! Maya is here!" she yelled to the hallway. "Would you like some tea, Maya?"

Mrs. Abadi's English had also been improving. Maya had invited her to join sessions with Sema when she was able to sit, which was not very often. It seemed that Mrs. Abadi was always cooking something fabulous, and today was no different.

As Maya sat down at the table, Mrs. Abadi offered her tea and a delicious cake. "This looks delicious!" praised Maya. "What is this?"

Sema joined them from the other room. "Eh dah, min fadlik?"

"Excuse me?" Maya looked confused.

"Eh dah, min fadlik? ... What is this, please?" laughed Sema. "It's Basbousa. Syrian cake. I will teach you how to make it, and how to say "Please" in Arabic."

"Okay. This sounds like a great lesson. We can work with recipes and measurements in English and Arabic today!" laughed Maya.
  Together the ladies got out the ingredients and made another cake. Maya learned how to make Basbousa, and Sema learned her fractions in English as she measured the ingredients. Maya also had her write the recipe in English.

Often their lessons progressed in this way. A conversation would spark a learning opportunity, and then Maya would help Sema with her homework before going home. Oddly enough, their lessons always seemed to promote their shared values of food, family, and fun!

During the month-long celebration of Ramadan, Sema taught Maya how to make fatteh, a traditional Syrian meal eaten for breakfast. Maya enjoyed learning more about Arabic and Islamic cultural traditions. In the beginning of their relationship, Sema had been hesitant to talk about problems she was having at school, but as they discovered shared values – including families, music and delicious food, the two young ladies built a foundation of relational trust[16].

As Maya and Sema's relationship evolved, Sema shared some of the challenges she was having at her school. Some of her classmates made fun of her culture, teasing her, because both Sema and her mother wore a hijab, a traditional head covering worn by many Muslim women. As Sema and Maya discussed ways to ameliorate the situation, Sema came up with the idea of having an International Day at school. Maya helped Sema organize the event by enlisting the help of one of the school guidance counselors and one of Sema's favorite teachers. Together, they created an International Day, inviting all the students in the school from different countries to talk about their culture and share information with the other students.

Maya had never planned an event like this, so, again, it became a learning experience for both of them. With the help of the school counselor and the teacher, Maya was able to contact five of Sema's classmates from China, Korea, Dominican Republic, Ethiopia, and Colombia, South America. Together, they worked hard with a team of volunteers to create decorations, food, and a PowerPoint presentation that acted as a travel guide, taking the students to each of their different countries. Sema's English teacher used the opportunity to have each student share about what they learned from the experience in class the following day. They even invited parents to participate

[16] Betty Neal Crutcher defines the cultivation of virtues as "the abilities and ways of knowing that enable one to deal with various personalities, cultures, and experiences — enables one to maintain individual and institutional boundaries, and to overcome barriers between people."

so they could hear the children communicate their different experiences. It became a learning experience for all, and helped create an appreciation for diversity.

Finally, both Maya and Sema's shared "vision" for this mentorship was helping Sema adapt and thrive in her new country and home, and, more specifically, to finish high school and prepare for her life afterwards as an American citizen. However, Sema's goals changed over the course of the mentorship, as new doors opened up to her, and as she learned what was truly available to her in her new home. What Maya had not expected, was the effect that the mentorship would have on her vision for her own future. She had learned so much in such a short time. Working with Sema had created a passion in her to work with other refugees, and she was considering changing her major.

The first week back at university, Maya scheduled an appointment with her advisor, Dr. Kelly Milo.

"Hi Maya! It's so good to see you! How was your summer?" asked Dr. Milo.

"Not long enough!" laughed Maya. "But I am also excited to get back to school and finish my studies!"

"How is your mentorship going at World Relief?"

"Excellent! I never dreamed I would learn so much. I thought I would be doing all the teaching, but Sema, my mentee, has taught me so much, and I've met so many people at her school. We've really worked as a team to help Sema succeed. That's why I wanted to see you today." Maya replied.

"Go on," encouraged Dr. Milo

"Well, I know it's my senior year, but I think I want to change my field of study."

"You do?" asked Dr. Milo

"Yes. I would like to find out more about immigration law, and how I can switch to pre-law. What classes do I need to take to pursue my studies in pre-law? I don't know if it's too late to change my schedule this semester, but we could at least start to look at next semester. Or perhaps I should start applying to law school?"

Dr. Milo could not help but smile. "It's amazing how mentoring can really change your life, isn't it Maya? I knew this would be a good opportunity for you. Let's take a look at your schedule now and see if we can't change a couple of things this semester, and then we'll look at the course catalogue for next semester. You may want to arrange a meeting with Dr. McKeehen, who is the department head for the School of Law. She also specializes in Immigration law, and can give you better advice on which classes to take, and how to proceed with law school. It may end up taking you longer to finish. Are you prepared for that?"

"Well, my finances might not be, but it's what I'd like to do," laughed Maya.

"Dr. McKeehen can also help you look into graduate assistantships and work study programs for financial assistance."

"Thank you so much, Dr. Kendall. I am really enjoying mentoring Sema. I think it has changed both of our lives in ways that we could never have imagined before."

INTEGRATION
Shared Learning in a Traditional Mentoring Relationship

In the case of Shawn and Anderson, Anderson learned many valuable tools and lessons from his mentee, Shawn. A few that should be highlighted for the sake of our conversation: communication skills, leadership skills, and updated technology and techniques.

The Mentor Learns Communication Skills

Through mentoring across distance, Anderson learned how to navigate the challenges of a remote learning environment, and improve and nurture his "long distance" relationship with his mentee. Learning to listen to Shawn's needs also helped Anderson develop a better sense of generosity and consideration for others, including those who worked under him in his own career. Because of the way he had left the mentorship the first time, he also learned how to work with his mentee to regain his trust – a very invaluable lesson, in view of the fact that EVERYONE makes mistakes in their relationships. **Being willing to examine one's own responsibilities for miscommunication, as well as improve communication skills with others, develops confidence and also strongly strengthens interpersonal relationships.**

The Mentor Learns Leadership Skills

Anderson learned from the mistake that he had made in not establishing a clear method of closure with Shawn the first time, when his new position required him to move across the country. He also learned how to reestablish and repair a relationship that he had damaged. Becoming a better mentor spilled over into Anderson's career, and also made him a better manager of people, of time (his schedule), and of his own career. The feeling of having let Shawn down the first time around did not sit well with Anderson. He truly wanted to become a better leader and mentor. Having the opportunity to improve those skills improved his own self-esteem.

The Mentor Learns Updated Technology and Techniques

Anderson knew that, while Shawn was learning from him how to develop experience in the field and navigate working in a global company, he was also learning more about the latest technology from Shawn's experience. Together, as a team, they both enhanced each other's performance.

The opportunity to mentor Shawn also provided Anderson with a chance to share his career experiences with a younger colleague in a more casual environment apart from his day-to-day office life. He found that his sessions with Shawn – both on the phone and in person – to be a welcome opportunity to share ideas and listen to, and learn from, the perspective of a younger colleague.

In the case of Sema and Maya, Sema also learned a great deal from her mentee as well. **The willingness of the mentor to learn from the mentee becomes crucial to the success of intercultural mentoring relationships.** In cross-cultural mentor-mentee dyads, there is a lot of give-and-take in the learning process. In addition, multi-cultural mentoring must be more communal and collaborative than traditional pairings. Mutual, shared learning is a key component. According to Cross-Cultural Mentoring consultant, Dr. Betty Neal Crutcher, "cross-cultural mentoring involves an ongoing, intentional, and mutually enriching relationship with someone of a different race, gender, ethnicity, religion, cultural background, socioeconomic background, sexual orientation, and/or nationality.

The Mentor Learns Communication Skills

When mentoring cross-culturally, language barriers have to be navigated, which presents a LEARNING experience in itself. In Maya's case, she took the time to learn at least a basic understanding of Arabic language and culture, and continued to grow in her experience of the language as she spent time with Sema and her family. She also had to become much clearer in her own speech and messaging in order to establish clear communication with her mentee.

The Mentor Learns Collaboration Skills

As seen in several examples of the mentoring relationships in this manual, mentoring often involves collaborating with others to provide the best learning experience for a mentee. Maya collaborated with Sema's teachers and guidance counselors to ease the transition for Sema at school. In doing so, Maya learned how to work with other professionals in the field toward a common goal of helping immigrant children succeed and thrive as they put down roots in their new communities.

Brushstrokes

The Mentor Learns Critical Thinking

Maya had to be open to new ways of teaching and sharing knowledge to meet her mentee's style of learning. Maya learned how to respond to the challenges that Sema was facing at school, and, together, they came up with a creative solution that benefitted not only Sema, but also other immigrant children in her school.

The Mentor Learns Cultural Appreciation

Another positive aspect of mentoring cross-culturally is developing an appreciation for diversity, the value of inclusion, and a greater respect for the challenges that newcomers to this country face.

In conclusion, mentoring a wide variety of mentees allows the mentor to continue LEARNING and adjusting to reach the needs of different mentees. For Mentor Maya, the mentorship engagement with Sema provided skills and experiences that certainly will be invaluable to her in her career, and also will enhance her resume as she graduates from college and enters the working world. For Mentor Anderson, the mentorship engagement with Shawn provided an excellent opportunity to increase his effectiveness working with his executive team members, and, in addition, with potential clients in the future.

CHAPTER SEVEN

LAUGHING

Laughter is a powerful tool that a mentor can utilize to soften the harsh realities that will inevitably exist in the life of the mentee.

"A sense of humor is part of the art of leadership, of getting along with people, of getting things done."
- Dwight D. Eisenhower

"He who laughs, lasts!"
- Mary Pettibone Poole

The person who has a sense of humor is not just more relaxed in the face of a potentially stressful situation, but is more flexible in his approach.
- John Morreall

"Enjoy the journey."
- Onnie Kirk, Jr.

The Prehistoric Pig Strikes Again

Mentor Joe pulled up to Isaiah's house overwhelmed with excitement about the events that he had planned for the day. After spending an entire month explaining to Isaiah about the details of money management, financial security saving and investing, it was finally time to put all that they had learned into action.

To start the adventure-packed day, Mentor Joe had planned to take Isaiah to the local bank and open Isaiah's first bank account. After opening the bank account, Joe had set up a mid-morning appointment with an investment broker, Ray Reeveson to further explain the ins and outs of investing in the stock market, bulls and bears, individual stock purchases, and mutual funds. The last stop of Joe's pre-planned, well-thought-out day was to visit a good friend named Fred McCrayson, who had made a living owning rental properties and purchasing apartment buildings. At the end of the day, Joe had hoped to integrate all that he had learned by showing Isaiah the concepts of rate of return and return on investment.

As Joe sat in his SUV, the door to Isaiah's house flung open and the young teenager emerged. As Isaiah stepped out of the house, closed the front door behind him, and slowly walked toward Joe's car, Joe could immediately sense that his well-laid plans were in substantial jeopardy. Isaiah's shoulders were slumped, his head hung low, and his lips were pressed tight as he shuffled his feet down the driveway. Isaiah opened the door and climbed into the front passenger seat. Immediately he collapsed into the passenger seat, slammed the door without eye-contact or a salutation, and clenched his fists as if he were about to fight Mike Tyson.

Joe paused for a moment, assessed the situation, withholding judgment, took a deep breath, and started in rather forcefully. "Isaiah, I am not sure what is going on in your life right now, but I need you to look me in the eye and answer this question." The momentary silence in the SUV seemed like an eternity as Isaiah fought through the rushing current of emotions that had flooded his psyche. Gathering himself and intentionally dismissing his usual tendency to withdraw, Isaiah mustered all of his strength and slowly raised his eyes to meet Joe's.

Joe knew that he would have to formulate his words precisely, and the tension in his SUV was intense. He took a deep breath and asked, "Isaiah, what do you call a prehistoric pig?"

Isaiah stared blankly into Joe's eyes, completely speechless. Joe did not wait for Isaiah's answer and quickly blurted out, "Jurassic Pork!"

Isaiah was flabbergasted because he had been hoodwinked, and struggled to keep a straight face. However, he could no longer keep it in. His rough exterior melted as he let out a high-pitched squeal that caught Joe completely off guard. Before they knew it, both mentor and mentee were laughing uncontrollably, and had been reduced to tears. A few minutes later, Joe pulled into the parking lot of the bank – having begun the day filled with laughter and amazement.

Laughter is strong medicine. It draws people together in ways that trigger healthy physical and emotional changes in the body. Laughter strengthens immune systems, boosts moods, diminishes pain, and protects from the damaging effects of stress. Nothing works faster or more dependably to bring one's mind and body back into balance than a good laugh.

Robinson, Smith and Seagal state, **"Humor lightens your burdens, inspires hope, connects you to others, and keeps you grounded, focused, and alert. It also helps you release anger and forgive sooner. With so much power to heal and renew, the ability to laugh easily and frequently is a tremendous resource for surmounting problems, enhancing your**

relationships, and supporting both physical and emotional health. Best of all, this priceless medicine is fun, free, and easy to use."

Joe's well-laid plans for the day had proven quite successful. As Joe and Isaiah left the site of one of Fred McCrayson's apartment buildings, Joe could not help but notice the huge smile on Isaiah's face. Joe and Isaiah climbed into the SUV.

"Hey, Isaiah, what was going on with you this morning? You did not look very good when you came out of your house," Joe inquired with trepidation – not sure if there was an active statute of limitations on Isaiah's volatile morning.

"Well, Mr. Joe, I stayed up late last night, and my Mom had to yell at me to get me out of bed. I really wanted to sleep in, but my Mom forced me to come with you today."

"How do you feel now?"

"I am so glad that I came today! This has been a great day. I think I might even go home and apologize to my Mom for being so stubborn and difficult."

Sema & Maya
It was the beginning of May, and almost the end of the semester for both Maya and Sema. They were still meeting once a week with Maya's adjusted school schedule. The days were getting longer and warmer, and Maya was looking forward to being able to take Sema to some fun places outside again. However, before their tutoring session, Maya got an unusual call from Mrs. Abadi. "Maya, we need to cancel Sema's class this week."

"Okay, Ms. Abadi. I hope Sema is okay?" Maya inquired.

"Maya, I cannot explain." ...There was a long pause. "Her Grandmother, my mother, ... has passed."

Maya didn't know what to say... "Allah yarhamha... I don't have the words to express my heartache. I am so sorry Mrs. Abadi. Thank you for telling me. Please let me know if I can be of any help."

A couple of days passed before Sema finally called Maya. When she arrived for her session, Sema was definitely not herself.

"Marhaba, Sema. How are you?

"Fine," Sema murmured in a low voice – not her usual bubbly self. Her posture was sunken. The two young women sat down at the kitchen table, while Sema's mother poured tea.

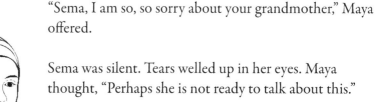

"Sema, I am so, so sorry about your grandmother," Maya offered.

Sema was silent. Tears welled up in her eyes. Maya thought, "Perhaps she is not ready to talk about this."

Mrs. Abadi rubbed her shoulders. "It will be okay, Sema. Show Maya your math homework. You know I cannot help you with it."

Sema pulled out her homework, and they began to look at the Trigonometry problems. After completing a few, it was clear that Sema's mind was elsewhere.

"Sema, tell me something about your grandma." Maya began... "Were you very close?"

"Yes," Sema answered. "But, of course, I have not seen her since we left Syria. It was not safe for her to travel with us. She has a heart condition. Or I guess that she had a heart condition." Sema gazed out the window. "Maya, it's still so hard for me to process. Just...I can't believe that she is not here anymore."

Sema paused before going on... "Being separated from family and friends is the hardest part. Some of them I know I will never see again. And so, it's bigger than just my Nanaa. It's everyone we left behind."

"I'm sorry, Sema. I cannot imagine what that is like." Maya took a deep breath, "What is your favorite memory of your grandmother?"

"Nanaa loved flowers...She especially loved poppies. She said that they made her laugh. My grandfather used to grow olives, and they had a field of poppies on their farm. I played there when I was very small – before the war.

Sema began to smile... "I remember one time, my parents were going into town, and they left me and my brother with Nanaa. She was making bread and watching me and my brother. We decided to play a joke on her. We were supposed to be helping with chores, but we sneaked out into the poppy field and hid. My brother was only 4 years old. I told him to lie down next to me in the poppies and be very still."

"I don't know how long it was before Nanaa realized we were missing, but it seemed like forever. When she found us, we thought she might be mad, but, instead, she was laughing so hard. She told us later that she had been very worried when she discovered us missing. When she went outside to look for us... she saw this... I don't know how you say it ...this "opening" in the field of poppies where we were both lying down with a pair of legs sticking out. They were my brother's. She laughed so hard that she cried. She still scolded us, but she couldn't stay angry for long. You should have seen her beautiful round face. She kept trying to be serious, but every time she tried, she would burst into laughter!"

Before long, Sema was laughing, thinking about how silly she and her brother must have looked with their shoes sticking out, hiding in the field of poppies.

Suddenly, Maya had an idea, "Sema, are you free on Saturday?"

"Um... I think so. Why?"

"I want to take you on a field trip," said Maya, smiling.

"I have to ask Mom, of course, and be home by dinner," said Sema.

On Saturday, Maya picked up Sema. Mrs. Abadi had packed them each a lunch. Maya brought bottles of water.

"So, where are we going?" Sema asked.

"You'll see!" Maya could barely contain her grin.

After about 40 minutes of driving, they headed away from the city – toward farmland. Maya pulled off at a particular exit. The scenery stretched out into open grassland.

"Sema, look out your window to the right." As Maya slowly pulled over into a clearing off the side of the road. Sema saw before her a field of poppies and other wildflowers that stretched as far as the eye could see.

She looked over at Maya... "What is this place?"

Maya said, "This is Mr. Onnie Kirk's Sonshine Farm, I used to pass it all the time on my way to a friend's house, and I always thought it was beautiful. I was hoping it was still here. Let's get out and explore."

Sema started to smile. "Maya, this is so beautiful. Thank you for bringing me here."

The two women got out of the car and started walking toward the flowers. Suddenly, Sema took off running right into the field, giggling and waving her arms in the air.

"This is just like Nanaa's!" she laughed.

Maya smiled. It was good to see her mentee feeling better.

Before they left, Maya had Sema lay down at the edge of the field with her feet sticking out of the end of the row. She took several pictures to capture the powerful image of a humorous memory of her Nanaa.

INTEGRATION

The Power of Laughter

Shared laughter is one of the most effective tools for keeping the mentoring relationship dynamic and progressive. All emotional sharing builds strong and lasting relationship bonds, but sharing laughter also adds joy, vitality, and resilience. Humor also unites people during difficult times, and is a powerful and effective way to heal resentments, disagreements, and hurts. Laughter can be a very potent weapon in the mentor's arsenal.

Humor and playful communication also strengthen the mentoring relationship by triggering positive feelings and fostering emotional connection. When a mentor and mentee share laughter with one another, a positive bond is created which acts as a strong buffer against stress, disagreements, and disappointment.

Laughter is an especially powerful tool for managing conflict and reducing tension when emotions are running high. Whether professionally or personally, mentors can learn to use humor to smooth over disagreements, lower everyone's stress level, and communicate in a way that builds up relationships, rather than breaking them down.

Mentors can often use laughter to diffuse very difficult situations that their mentee might encounter. As everyone knows, life is not easy – especially as the landscape of one's life becomes more and more complex; however, one overarching principle remains: Laughter is medicine.

Brushstrokes

Laughter is an incredible gift. It is the birthright of both the mentor and the mentee, and is a natural part of life that is innate and inborn. Infants begin smiling during the first weeks of life, and laugh within just months of being born. Even if a mentor and a mentee had not grown up in households in which laughter was common, they can learn to laugh at any stage of life, and incorporate it into the content of the mentor engagement.

Even if, up to a given point of time, a person has experienced a stress-filled, "low-laughter" life, they can begin to turn things around by simply setting aside special times to break out of their normal, tedious routine in order to seek out humor and laughter. Also, even exercise can be an extremely effective stress-reducer. Eventually, such a person will want to incorporate humor and laughter into the fabric of their life, and, ultimately, will enjoy finding humor and laughter naturally in virtually everything!

A Mentor Should Smile with Their Mentee

Smiling is the beginning of laughter, and, like laughter, it is contagious. Just like Joe and Isaiah, when a person looks at someone and sees something even mildly pleasing or humorous, that person should practice smiling, instead of looking down at their phone. In addition, they should look up and smile at people that they pass in the street, and at the person serving their morning coffee, and at the co-workers with whom they share an elevator. Also, one would benefit from developing the habit of studying the powerful effect that their smiles have on others, especially if the smiles are accompanied by spoken words – because such feedback would help develop an even larger repertoire of spoken verbiage, as well as special body language for different situations.

A Mentor Should Count Their Blessings with Their Mentee
A mentor should make a physical list of the positive aspects of their life viz-a-viz their mentee, and also share that list with their mentee. Such a simple act will help distance their mentee from negative thoughts that often block humor and laughter. When a person is sad, they have to travel further to reach humor and laughter.

People who hear laughter, move toward it. Sometimes, humor and laughter are private, such as a shared joke among a small group, but, usually, jokes are not private. More often than not, people are very happy to share something funny because it gives them an opportunity to laugh again, and feed off that humor. When one hears laughter, they should seek it out and ask, "What's funny?"

Introduce Your Mentee to Fun, Playful People
These should be people who, despite their executive positions, laugh easily – both at themselves, and at life's absurdities; these are the people who routinely find the humor in everyday events. Their playful point of view and laughter are contagious. Even if one does not consider themself to be a lighthearted, humorous person, they can still seek out people who like to laugh and make others laugh. Every comedian appreciates an audience.

Bring Humor Into The Conversation
Ask your mentee, "What's the funniest thing that happened to you today? This week? In your life?" Initially, this question will produce an awkward silence because people have been trained to focus on the negative, or on the things that are wrong. Subsequently, a mentee may find it very difficult to turn their attention to the positive. Over time, however, both mentor and mentee will begin to develop an eye for the humorous things in life, and both will be better for it.

Mentors who have the ability to laugh, play, and have fun not only make the mentoring relationship more enjoyable, but they also help their mentee to solve problems, connect with others, and think more creatively. Mentors who incorporate humor and play into their interactions find that it continually renews not only themselves, but also their mentoring relationship.

Life seems to usually bring challenges that can either get the best of one's mentee, or become negative scenarios that flood the mentee's imagination. When a mentor becomes "a problem," and takes themself too seriously, it can be hard to think outside of the box and find new solutions. But, when a person plays with a problem, they often can transform "the problem" into an opportunity for creative learning. Playing with problems seems to come naturally to children. When they are confused or afraid, children make their problems into a game, which gives them a sense of control, and an opportunity to experiment with new solutions. Similarly, interacting with others in playful ways helps an adult to retain and even improve upon such creative abilities. As my mentor Onnie Kirk says, "Enjoy the journey!"

CHAPTER EIGHT

LOVING

Love is not just a four-letter word, and to be successful, the mentor must understand the concept of unconditional positive regard.

"What counts in life is not the mere fact that we have lived.
It is what difference we have made to the lives of others that will determine the significance of the life we lead."
- Nelson Mandela

"I am an example of what is possible when girls from the very beginning of their lives are loved and nurtured by people around them. I was surrounded by extraordinary women in my life who taught me about quiet strength and dignity."
- Michelle Obama

"Those who truly care for you will linger, accept, and understand you."
- Mayra Betances

"Blaze a trail that will help others begin their journey, and it will never be lonely at the top."
- Carlos Wallace

A Personal Question

"Alexandra, can I ask you a question?" Rena opened the meeting.

Alexandra paused for a moment, and then looked into Rena's eyes. She was not sure what she was going to get.

"Alexandra Milner-Middlebrooks, you are an incredibly effective supervisor and team leader. You also are a powerful motivator, and an equally effective mentor. I have grown so much in the few short months that you have served as my mentor. Coming into this new job at Strategion and this mentorship program, I never would have imagined that I would have made these leaps and bounds personally and professionally. So, I am interested and intrigued. Here is my question: 'in your personal view, what makes you so effective as a leader, and, more importantly, as a mentor? What is your secret to success?'"

Sipping her morning coffee, Alexandra was a little caught off guard by Rena's line of questioning so early in the morning. Fortunately, however, over the last several months, she had grown accustomed to Rena Briellen's deep, insightful probing questions. She pondered for a moment, took another sip of Columbian blend, inhaled deeply, and began to speak.

"I must admit that I was not expecting our session to begin like this, but I will give your question an unpolished, unpoliticized, unplanned response." Alexandra quickly thought over her many years of leadership and professional development, and then spoke confidently and assertively.

"Rena, I truly believe that my effectiveness and specifically my success as a mentor, can be boiled down into three simple letters. I really try to approach each individual, each interaction, each meeting, each moment, and every occasion with these three letters in mind."

Rena sat on the edge of her seat. She knew that she was entering a sacred space.

Alexandra continued building suspense, "I strongly feel that these three letters essentially provide the foundation and framework for successful mentorship."

Rena could sense that Alexandra was dramatically milking the moment, and began wringing her hands in suspenseful animation, "Well...?" Alexandra continued, speaking slowly for dramatic effect, "Rena, my powerful protégé, my magnificent mentee, I don't share these three letters with just anyone. If I share these three precious letters with you, are you going to cherish them and guard them with your very life?"

Rena was now genuinely intrigued. "Yes! Yes! I promise!"

Alexandra leaned in, "U.P.R."

Rena laughed, looked puzzled, and continued to play in Alexandra's screenplay. "U.P.R.? Really? What is that?"

Alexandra smiled and, after taking a sip of joe, "U.P.R. are the initials for **Unconditional Positive Regard**."

Rena looked intrigued, "Ok, my guru, I am listening."

"Well, I stumbled across the concept of "unconditional positive regard" while doing some research on workplace dynamics and culture. It's actually a clinical term; however, my laywoman's definition is... **the attitude of complete acceptance and love, whether for yourself or for someone else**."

Alexandra continued, **"When you have unconditional positive regard for someone, nothing they can do could give you a reason to stop seeing them as inherently human and inherently lovable."**

Rena leaned in, "Inherently human and inherently lovable? Are you serious? Does this always work? I've got some co-workers whose humanity I constantly question!"

Alexandra continued, "It does not mean that you accept each and every action taken by the person, but that you accept who they are at a level much deeper than surface behavior. I have found that, when I approach each individual and each interaction with unconditional positive regard, it allows me to put my interaction, and the purposes for my interaction, into crystal clear perspective. This most certainly applies to my role as a supervisor and a mentor – especially when I show up for, and participate in, business meetings, team huddles, and even my interactions with you."

Rena was still processing, "U.P.R. I see. Unconditional positive regard."

Another Perspective

Isaiah ran out of his house with a big smile on his face and an even bigger box sloppily coated with wrapping paper and a huge red bow. The young, lanky teenager, whose height had now reached six foot three inches, jumped into Joe's SUV and planted the ornamental box firmly in Joe's lap.

"Here Mr. Joe!" Isaiah's short stature had definitely departed, but his jovial childlike personality had remained.

Joe looked at Isaiah's white, flashy, brilliant smile, "What's this for, young warrior?"

"Ahhhhhh, Mr. Joe! C'mon! It's for you. Open it! I picked it out and wrapped it all by myself."

"I definitely can tell that you wrapped it!" Joe's comment went over Isaiah's head. Joe slowly opened the box, and immediately looked away in an attempt to hide the tears that instantaneously began to fill his eyes. Quickly composing himself, Joe unfolded the sweat-shirt emblazoned with the words "Hampton University."

"Mr. Joe! What is wrong with your eyes? What is that wet stuff running down your face? Are you ok? Do I need to call the waaaaaaambulance?" he joked.

Isaiah was ruthless and would never pass up the rare opportunity to heckle his mentor. Further taking advantage of the moment, he continued, "Do you need me to run back into the house and get a box of tissues?"

Joe playfully slugged Isaiah in the arm. "What's this young man?"

"I've been accepted to Hampton University!" Isaiah exclaimed, unable to contain his excitement.

"This is incredible, Isaiah! This is the best news that I have had in quite some time." Joe discreetly tried to wipe the moisture from his eyes, but it was too late. Isaiah would never let him live this one down.

"Well, Mr. Joe, I just wanted you to be the first to know, and I also wanted you to know how much I appreciate you mentoring me for the last three years. I know that it has not been easy, and that there were times that I really got on your nerves! How did you put up with me?"

Joe looked at Isaiah, "Do you really want to know?"

"Of course, Mr. Joe! How did you do it?"

"U.P.R., my son. U.P.R." Joe smiled.

"U.P.R? Upper? What are you talking about Mr. Joe?"

"Well Isaiah, as you know, I have been around the block a couple of times but in one of our mentor training sessions, we learned the concept of unconditional positive regard, and it has formed the foundation for all of our interactions. You see, Isaiah, when I first met you, I knew that we would encounter rough patches and many opportunities for growth, but I always viewed you through the lens of unconditional positive regard."

Isaiah was transfixed.

"Isaiah, **unconditional positive regard** is not something that you earn or have to work for. You don't have to dance a certain way, dress a certain way, talk a certain way, or do anything special to be special. You don't have to have a certain score on your SAT, and you don't have to rush for 100 yards each game for me to acknowledge your unique giftedness – that is, you are inherently human and inherently lovable. I hate to admit it, though!" Joe joked.

Isaiah smiled once again, and immediately started laughing. "So, what you are really saying, Mr. Joe. Is it that you love me? You can tell me. I won't make fun of you."

INTEGRATION

Yes, there definitely is a "secret sauce" that is the main ingredient in The Art of Effective Mentoring. As mentioned in the introduction, this secret sauce is what distinguishes mentoring from the other disciplines, such as coaching, teaching, or counseling. I would venture to say that the main ingredient in this secret sauce is the transformational power of unconditional positive regard.

Carl Rogers, described unconditional positive regard as: "...caring for the client, but not in a possessive way or in such a way as simply to satisfy the therapist's own needs... It means caring for the client as a separate person, with permission to have his own feelings, his own experiences" (Rogers, 1957).

According to Rogers, problematic behaviors like overeating, drinking too much, and procrastinating aren't altered with confrontation, judgment, or punishment; rather, they are remedied with compassion, understanding, and acceptance.

Hard Wired for Actualization Achievement

In Rogers' view, people are wired for self-actualization, or the need to fulfill potential. However, painful experiences like abandonment by a parent, or being bullied, shamed, or being negatively judged tend to thwart people's growth. Therefore, for The Art of Effective Mentoring, it can be stated that the mentor should first understand that their protégé is hard-wired for achievement and self-actualization – both personally and professionally. Within the mentee, although sometimes dormant, is the need for self-actualization – that is, the opportunity and environment to fulfill the dreams that are lying deep within them. An environment of unconditional positive regard provides a powerful incubator for human self-actualization.

Hard Wired for Authenticity

Second, the mentor should realize that unconditional positive regard is the foundational principle that encourages and empowers the mentee to evolve into his or her true authentic self. It restores the mentee's hope by showing them that their unique gifts, talents, personalities, and idiosyncrasies are loved and accepted. From Roger's lens, when a mentee feels safe, honesty follows. And being honest with oneself and with others is crucial for change.

How to Incorporate Unconditional Positive Regard
UPR - Mentee Thoughts & Feelings

One of the best representations of unconditional positive regard in mentoring sessions is a common scenario in which the mentee shares thoughts, feelings, and/or behaviors with the mentor that are considered by the public at large to be morally wrong, or simply unacceptable. In this case, the mentor can display unconditional acceptance and unconditional positive regard by asking their mentee about their own feelings, and what they believe drove the thought or behavior – rather than focusing on how the mentee's actions would hurt someone else, or on the illegality or immorality of the action.

UPR - Mentee Habits, Actions & Behaviors

For another example, therapists have the opportunity to display unconditional positive regard when a client shares a habit or behavior with them that is self-detrimental or self-harmful, such as abusing drugs or alcohol, cutting, or binge-eating. Instead of chiding the client for this behavior, or ignoring its potential to harm, the therapist might help the client realize that the behavior is harmful – while simultaneously assuring the client that they are worthy of love and selfcare, and that they deserve to have a healthy and happy life.

UPR - Mentee Modeling

Finally, unconditional positive regard can be seen in the mentor's modeling of acceptance to the mentee. The unconditionally accepting mentor will show the protégé that he is still accepted and valued, even when he makes mistakes. The mentor's positive regard works as a model for the mentee's acceptance of himself and those around him. In other words, this UPR modeling gives the mentee the powerful picture that, if the mentor can accept him, no matter what he does, he can also accept himself, his coworkers, and everyone else with whom he might come in contact.

Brushstrokes

Having an attitude of UPR toward a protégé can encourage them to share their thoughts, feelings, and behaviors more openly with the mentor. A protégé who is afraid that the mentor will be shocked, offended, or judgmental will likely not be very forthcoming with any information that they feel may be perceived as negative or unacceptable. Of course, this withholding of important information can have a very negative impact on the mentoring relationship and, in turn, on any personal or professional improvements that the protégé is looking to gain from the mentoring engagement.

It has been suggested that unconditional positive regard from the mentor may be a substitute for the unconditional positive regard that the protégé did not receive from their parents or other important adults in their childhood and professional journey. Carl Rogers believed that those who do not receive such regard from their parents at a young age are more likely to have low self-worth, and less likely to reach their full potential with regards to personal development. This theory is critical to keep in mind during mentoring sessions and throughout the mentoring engagement. (Good Therapy, 2015).

UPR, Feelings and Forward Thinking

When a mentee comes to a mentor with an admission – whether personally or professionally – that can be viewed negatively or as a set-back, this is an excellent opportunity to practice unconditional positive regard.
The opposite response would be to show disdain, disappointment, or even to get upset. In such moments, all of us can remember being chastised, corrected, or disciplined; such corrective methods tend to over-focus on past performance, and seldom result in forward focus or lasting change.

Instead of giving in to the urge to focus on what a mentee has done wrong, a mentor should try to focus on the mentee's feelings, and be forward thinking. This would be especially important if a mentee came to a mentor with an admission of guilt, or a request for advice. A mentor should ask the mentee how he/she feels about their actions, and allow the mentee to formulate their own game plan toward making better decisions as life moves forward.

UPR and a Mentor's Attitude

To cultivate an attitude of unconditional positive regard for their mentee, a mentor should remind themself of some simple truths. A mentor can repeat these sayings as a twist on the usual self-focus of mantras or affirmations:

- "My protégé's worth is non-negotiable, and does not need to be earned."
- "I approve of my protégé without condition, although I may not approve of all the choices my protégé has made, or will make in the future."
- "I give my protégé permission to make mistakes, and I believe in his/her ability to learn from them."
- "I believe in my protégé's ability to become who they are meant to be."
- "I am here to help, understand, and provide guidelines — not to criticize."

(Adapted from McMahon, 2013)

For more great references on Unconditional Positive Regard, see:

https://www.psychologytoday.com/us/blog/what-doesnt-killus/201210/unconditional-positive-regard - Dr. Stephen Joseph: "What is Unconditional Positive Regard in Psychology?" Courtney E. Ackerman,

MSc. https://positivepsychology.com/unconditional-positiveregard/

SECTION

THE FINISHING TOUCHES

THE FINISHING TOUCHES

The finishing touches are critical for every masterpiece and the mentoring engagement is no exception. This section consists of one chapter that focuses on three concepts that should inform or form the concluding stages of every mentoring relationship.

- LANDING
- LAUNCHING
- LIONISING

LANDING encourages the mentoring program and the mentor to evaluate all phases of the mentoring engagement from both the mentor and the mentee's perspectives.

LAUNCHING invites the mentor to use his/her resources to propel the mentee into productivity and purpose.

LIONIZING prompts the mentor to promote and connect his/her mentee with a network of professionals who will ensure the mentee's success.

CHAPTER NINE

LANDING, LAUNCHING & LIONIZING

The mentoring relationship can ultimately provide the fuel that launches the mentee into a universe of unlimited possibilities.

"You need to assess yourself on a yearly basis and see how far you have gone, and what you still need to work on"
- Sunday Adelaja

"Assessment pushes instruction by stressing the importance of critical thinking, reasoning, and reflection, thus creating a quality learning environment."
- Richard Fletcher

"The price of success is hard work, dedication to the job at hand, and the determination that whether we win or lose, we have applied the best of ourselves to the task at hand."
- Vince Lombardi, Hall of Fame coach

Anderson & Shawn

It had been a year since Shawn and Anderson had resurrected their mentoring agreement. Despite the initial setbacks and challenges, the mentor and protégé successfully navigated the usual highs and lows, ins and outs, ups and downs, and were able to maintain a fairly consistent mentoring schedule. Only a few of their Zoom meetings had to be rescheduled, and the quarterly trips to Seattle had become a welcome respite as Shawn became acclimated to his new position with Delta Strategies.

Even with the initial difficulties of their mentorship engagement, from outward appearances, Troy Robbs sensed that the relationship had proven quite beneficial for Shawn and equally so for Anderson. Notwithstanding, Troy knew that it was always the best practice to conduct year-end assessments and evaluations to get a true picture of the success of all mentoring relationships.

As the Executive Director for Executive Mentoring Services, Troy provided Anderson with a fifteen question assessment in order to evaluate his mentoring engagements with Shawn.

- *Was a written plan established by the mentee at the beginning – including goals to be met under the mentor's direction or guidance?*
- *Were the guidelines established at the beginning: defining how often and/or when the mentee would meet on a routine basis?*
- *Did the mentor and mentee determine at the beginning of the relationship, guidelines by which to evaluate the success of the relationship?*
- *Was your mentee easy to approach and talk with?*
- *Did you and your mentee achieve satisfactory progress toward the goals planned?*
- *Did/does your mentee accept advice and encouragement from you with respect to your independent goals?*
- *Did/do the two of you meet regularly (monthly or quarterly)?*

- *Were you happy with the frequency and style of mentoring in your relationship?*
- *Did/do you provide regular feedback and constructive criticism?*
- *Did you facilitate your mentee's participation in professional activities outside of his place of employment (regional, state, and national organizations)?*
- *Did you involve your mentee in networking?*
- *Did you introduce your mentee to people at work and/or in the community?*
- *Did you connect your mentee to other senior professionals who could "fill in the gaps" in areas in which you might be less skilled?*
- *Did you observe your mentee in an executive context, and provide feedback on these critical skills?*
- *Did the relationship meet your expectations?*

At the conclusion of their first year, Troy had asked both Shawn and Anderson to complete his company's standard annual mentoring evaluation form. One form was designated for the mentor (aforementioned on the previous page), and another form designated for the mentee. The purpose of the tools was not only to collect important feedback from both the mentor and the mentee, but also to provide quantitative and qualitative data to support the program's efficacy.

The data generated by mentor and mentee feedback had also proven essential in Troy's efforts to secure sponsors and recruit executive level mentors for his mentoring company. Finally, Troy often used his clients' feedback and exit interviews to create videos, articles, brochures, and other promotional material to market his company, Executive Mentoring Solutions.

In addition, as another evaluative instrument to commemorate Anderson and Shawn's anniversary, Troy hosted a Zoom call with both mentor and protégé in an attempt to observe the dynamics of their interaction.
- *Was their conversation supportive and encouraging?*

- *Were both parties mutually engaged?*
- *Were there any passive aggressive comments or remarks?*
- *Were both parties satisfied with the progression of the mentee's personal and professional development plan?*

And even though Troy had made periodic calls throughout the course of the year (to touch base with Anderson and Shawn individually), it was his company's practice to conduct these annual in-person reviews to ensure the health and success of all of their mentor-mentee matches.

"How are you two doing?" Troy began.

"I think we are doing pretty well!" Shawn started eagerly, but immediately paused and proceeded carefully – trying not to speak presumptuously. "How do you think we are doing Anderson?"

Anderson chimed in, acknowledging Shawn's course correction, "I wholeheartedly agree with you Shawn! I think we are doing well. I feel like we have made considerable progress toward our goals, and that we have been extremely disciplined and proactive with all of our strategies."

Troy wanted to dive deeper, "On a scale from one to ten, how would you rate your mentoring relationship in terms of meeting your personal expectations? Anderson, I would like to hear your thoughts first."

"Well Troy, as you know, as a fairly new mentor, I wasn't quite sure what to expect. After we established our goals and benchmark strategies, my expectations became much more discernible and focused. Having explicit goals really helped me position myself to effectively mentor Shawn. It also allowed me to identify and further clarify my role. Or should I say roles?"

"What do you mean?" Troy was curious.

"Well...some days, based upon the mood and the conversation, I would relate with Shawn as a wise old owl; I just simply asked questions, and allowed Shawn to arrive at his own understandings. Other days, I would relate to Shawn like Morpheus, encouraging Shawn to dream bigger, to envision greater realities, and not to sell himself short."

Troy was appreciative of Anderson's attention to detail and transparency.

Anderson paused and continued to explain, "Oddly enough, over the last several months, I have sort of felt like a calm, patient, old golden retriever – by just providing Shawn with loving, honest feedback, and companionship as he worked through the nuances and ramifications of his choices. I have intentionally made it a point to remind Shawn of my unconditional positive regard toward him as he steps into the next powerful phase of his career."

"Troy, to get back to your initial question, going into the mentoring relationship, I was not sure what to expect, but, after a month or so, I realized that my roles as a mentor often were directly correlated with providing Shawn with the specific support that he needed at the time – with the ultimate purpose being his achieving his personal and professional goals. I would give our relationship a 9.5 – understanding that there are always opportunities for improvement"

"Wow. That was very profound." Troy was pleasantly surprised, and quite pleased that Anderson had embraced his significance as a mentor. It was apparent that Anderson had thoughtfully considered the technical aspects of effective mentorship, as well as his own ability and responsibility to play a pivotal role in his mentee's personal and professional development.

Troy continued, "What about you Shawn? Anderson just put it out there. How about you? Were your expectations met?"

"You know, it is very interesting to hear Anderson share, especially with me in the room..." Shawn smiled, reached out, and patted Anderson on the shoulder.

Everyone laughed.

"But I really feel as if my expectations began to morph as the year progressed."

"How so?" Troy's interest was piqued because he hadn't expected such a response.

"Well, when Anderson and I began with setting my goals, I expected our relationship to be very transactional. I was expecting to rely heavily on Anderson to hold me accountable, and to recommend the various resources that I would need to achieve those goals. I really expected Anderson to be my "coach" – similar to my basketball coach in high school, providing me with the skills, offensive plays, and defensive plays that I would need to win in the professional game."

Shawn leaned in. "It's funny. Not only did Anderson meet my expectations in those areas rather easily, but I began to notice that our interactions became much more transformational for me. Anderson was more than a Socrates, Morpheus, or basketball coach; over the course of the past year, Anderson really became a mentor to me. I can't really put my finger on anything specific, other than going back to the words transactional and transformational. Over the course of the year, I appreciated our transactions and the exchanging of information, but I really valued how transformative our mentoring relationship had become."

Shawn paused and the room went silent. They all recognized the sacred space that had just been established.

"Thanks, Shawn." Anderson was visibly moved by Shawn's words.

Troy paused, "Well gentlemen, from observing your interaction, it appears that this year has been absolutely horrible!" (He said, tongue-in-cheek.) "Just kidding! It's quite obvious that you are doing well. I appreciate your honest and heartfelt feedback. At this point, I will encourage you to review your mentoring contract to determine if you would like to continue with the terms in your mentoring agreement, or to make changes. For example, determine if you would like to relax the requirements, or completely end the formality of your weekly check-ins and quarterly in-persons. I encourage both of you to be open and honest about your commitments, and the feasibility of maintaining your existing agreement. Please let me know what you decide. I will be reaching out to you individually as well. Do you have any questions for me? If not, I am going to have to leave because I have another Zoom call at 2pm."

Shawn laughed, "The only question I have is, "When are you going to fly Anderson and me to Nashville for some hot wings?"

Alexandra the Mentor
and
Rena the Mentee

Strategion's mentoring program only called for a one-year commitment, and the company also required, near the end of the year, Alexandra and Rena to conduct an assessment to evaluate the effectiveness of their corporate mentoring program. In addition to the assessment, Strategion also administered individual exit surveys for both the mentee and the protégé.

Alexandra (The Mentor) was asked survey questions such as...
1. *Describe what best describes your relationship with your mentee. Very close? Close? Not very close? Explain.*
2. *Describe what best describes the success of your mentoring engagement. Very successful? Successful? Not very successful?*
3. *Did you feel that you received adequate support and supervision from Strategion's program staff?*
4. *What aspects of Strategion's Mentoring Program did you like the best?*
5. *What aspects of Strategion's Mentoring Program did you like the least?*
6. *What could Strategion have done to make our program a better experience for you and/or your mentee?*

7. *Would you like to be rematched?*

Rena (The Mentee) was asked questions such as...
1. *Describe what best describes your relationship with your mentor. Very close? Close? Not very close? Explain.*
2. *Describe what best describes the success of your mentoring engagement. Very successful? Successful? Not very successful?*
3. *Were you satisfied with your mentoring engagement?*
4. *Did you feel as if your mentor supported your professional development goals?*
5. *What professional development milestones and/or goals did you achieve with the assistance of your mentor?*
6. *Was Strategion's Mentoring Program effective in helping you progress in your career?*

Rena sat down in Alexandra's office for their final "official" mentoring meeting.

Alexandra handed Rena a nicely wrapped gift. "Alexandra! What are you doing? You shouldn't have done this!" Rena said.

"Just open it!" Alexandra giggled.

Rena began to unwrap the gift slowly and delicately. Rena's meticulous and methodical technique for opening gifts was more than Alexandra could bear. Alexandra anxiously watched for a few seconds and could not stand to be tortured further. She jumped up, grabbed the box, and ripped the rest of the wrapping paper off the box. As she threw the final remnants of paper onto the floor, it revealed a beautifully crafted French press coffee maker, and an assorted supply of coffee beans from around the world.

Alexandra screamed in delight, "Now you can stop stealing my coffee!" Rena began to tear up, but Alexandra would have nothing of it.

"Stop it! You are acting like we are never going to see each other again! Might I remind you that your office is only thirty steps down the hall and past the elevator?"

"I know, Alexandra. I know. But you have made my first year at Strategion the absolute best year of my career. I have learned so much, and you have single handedly motivated me in so many different areas of my life. My core, my craft, my career, my community, my compartments – in all of these areas, I have been able to define and progress toward my goals and..."

Alexandra interrupted, "OK! OK! But what I must know for my personal betterment is specifically what sessions and interactions had the most positive impact for you?"

Rena took a moment to gather her thoughts. "Definitely one of the most effective interactions and strategies that you utilized was our goal setting session, and the subsequent follow ups. These sessions really helped me drill down into my personal motivations, and where I would like to see myself at various stages in my career. Then, when we isolated the specific, quantifiable, interim steps that would accelerate me toward the long range goals, I was finally able to begin moving the needle toward well-conceived specifics for my career plans. And thanks for holding me accountable!"

"I also love that you were able to translate the theoretical principles into practical and quantifiable measures that I could implement immediately. I now see myself as a much more capable person. I am much more confident and comfortable with who I am now, and the unique talent that I bring to our company – thanks to your help and direction."

Alexandra jotted down a few of Rena's remarks in her journal, and continued to listen.

"The second strategy that had a very positive and meaningful effect was our off-site reflection sessions. I absolutely loved our working lunches at the Brown Mustache café, during which you encouraged me to examine my recent experiences, and to dive deep into life-learning lessons. During these briefings, you really helped me isolate, identify, and interpret my feelings. You also challenged me to further develop forward- thinking skills, and you modeled how to proactively use my past experiences as growth and learning opportunities. Alexandra, I am forever grateful!"

Joe the Mentor
and
Isaiah the Mentee

As Isaiah made final plans to attend Hampton University, Joe took advantage of every possible opportunity to ensure that his protégé had the professional connections he needed to be successful. Reaching out to old fraternity brothers, colleagues, professors, and administrators, Joe arranged for several introductory calls and in-person meetings so that his young protégé would immediately have access to a plethora of resources once he set foot on campus.

Joe also helped Isaiah set up a professional LinkedIn profile that included his part-time job, his summer internship, his volunteer work, his anticipated degree, and projected graduation date from Hampton University. Within a few weeks, Joe had introduced and successfully connected Isaiah with over one-hundred professionals on the social media platform.

With every meeting, Joe continued to remind Isaiah of the old adage, **"It is not what you know, but who you know!"**

Joe also emphasized the critical importance of his local village, and assured his young mentee that the connections in his personal and professional network could later become powerfully valuable resources to leverage should any challenges arise – not to mention, a well-established network that could open the door for future possibilities and opportunities. Over the last three years, as Isaiah had gotten older and matured, he had become increasingly attentive and receptive to Joe's mentoring messages. Isaiah's attentiveness had heightened as he realized that his relationship with Joe would change significantly when he moved away.

Since Isaiah planned to play football and major in Sports Management, Joe set up a lunch appointment with Correy Hudson, a good friend who also attended Hampton, and who had earned a master's degree in Sports Management. Although Joe began the lunch with a warm initial introduction, he purposefully scheduled another appointment – leaving Isaiah to fend for himself. He had coached Isaiah about the importance of making good first impressions, the opening handshake, the elevator speech, and the importance of making small talk. Joe had also reminded him of the importance of closing the meeting by exchanging contacts and social media addresses, various next steps, and how to end the meeting with forward-facing action items.

Isaiah showed up for his meeting with Correy with a fresh haircut and the tailored blazer that Joe had gotten him as a graduation present. Isaiah shook Correy's hand firmly, made eye-contact, and followed the game plan succinctly with care and enthusiasm, and then shared his aspirations for football and a subsequent career in sports management.

As the calendar year for the mentoring program wound down, to further facilitate closure, the mentoring program conducted an annual Rites of Passage ceremony for all of its graduating seniors.

Maya graduated from college and was accepted into Yale. Sema was heartbroken to find out that Maya would be relocating. As a result, Maya wanted to ensure that their mentor-mentee relationship would continue.

Maya felt a mix of emotions as she drove to Sema's house for their last mentoring session of the school year, and their one-year evaluation with the World Relief Organization. It didn't seem like an entire year had passed since they had first met, and Sema had come a long way in such a short time. Maya remembered how shy and frightened she had seemed at first. Now, she was excelling in school, playing on the women's soccer team, a member of the Honor Society, and considering her choices upon graduation. Cheryl Saylor, the mentorship program director for World Relief Organization, was also meeting with them and with Mrs. Abadi.

When Maya arrived, Cheryl Saylor was already there – enjoying Mrs. Abadi's signature tea and cake, and chatting with Sema and her mom.

Maya the Mentor
and
Sema the Mentee

"Good afternoon Maya," Mrs. Saylor greeted her as Mrs. Abadi poured her some tea. "How's everything?"

"I have some news." Maya couldn't suppress her smile. "Sema already knows – I spoke with her on the phone last night, because I didn't want to surprise her at the meeting."

"Well, what is it?" asked Mrs. Saylor. "Don't keep us in suspense!"

She looked at Sema and then back to Maya.

"I was accepted into Yale Law School," Maya answered. "I'll be moving in the fall."

"Well, that's exciting! Congratulations, Maya! I didn't know that you were considering law school." Mrs. Saylor paused... "I guess this means that you won't be mentoring with us next fall."

"Yes." Maya's smile faded. "That's the sad part. At least, I won't be able to meet with Sema on a weekly basis. But we did talk about remaining connected and doing virtual meetings."

Mrs. Saylor looked over at Sema, "How do you feel about this Sema? Part of this evaluation is to look at your goals and see what you have achieved, and whether or not you wish to continue with your mentorship."

"Well, I'm a little sad," Sema answered. "I am going to miss my Thursday night sessions with Maya. But I am really very happy for her. She deserves this..."

"No one said that we have to stop our sessions completely, Sema! Remember, we discussed last night the possibility of FaceTime once a month to see how you are doing!" encouraged Maya.

Sema nodded, and Mrs. Saylor took the lead again, "Sema, how do you feel about that? Would you like to continue? We can also find you another mentor here if you prefer."

"I am okay with this, Mrs. Saylor. When Maya told me last night, I was honestly heartbroken at first. But I am doing really well in school now. Maya's sessions have helped tremendously. I could still use some help next year, especially with test prep, and I was hoping Maya might be around to suggest schools for me to apply to for college."

"I can still do that, Sema. I can show you some test prep resources online, and if you have any problem understanding anything FaceTime will be our friend. I will also be visiting home in the spring, and we can definitely look at some colleges then if you like."

"Okay. Honestly, next year feels so far off. I just want to enjoy the summer before you leave!"

"Sema, tell me more about your mentorship experience. Can you elaborate on what worked, and what we could have done better?" asked Mrs. Saylor. "How do you feel going into your senior year? Do you feel like you want to continue with the program?" asked Mrs. Saylor.

"Mrs. Saylor, I feel like I am doing much better with school now. But I also do not want to say good-bye to Maya. She is like part of my family. This mentorship has been invaluable to me, Mrs. Saylor. Maya went beyond expectations to help not only me, but also made my family feel welcome and confident. I don't know how I could have gotten through the school year without her. I have been able to keep my grades up. It was really hard having to study English, and complete all of my assignments, but Maya's assistance made it easier. No question, I could not have done as well without her help!"

Mrs. Saylor continued, "Looking back at the personal goals that you set out to achieve at the beginning of the mentorship, where are you now on that personal journey? "

"When I came here, it was very hard for me. – I wasn't even sure what my goals were, except that my parents wanted me to finish school. I was so overwhelmed. I wanted to fit in, which I guess every kid wants. We left my friends and my cousins back in Syria. Everything is very different here. My father had spent some time here some years ago, but none of the rest of my family had ever been outside of Syria. My father always said good things about America – about coming here. But, when we got here, many people were not so friendly toward foreigners."

I think most people who have not had to leave their country cannot imagine what it is like – cannot put themselves in your shoes. Maya told me that her family had moved a lot when she was little, so I think that she had a better idea about how hard it is to move your school, leave your friends, make new friends, and even make a new life. Her family did not move because of war, but she at least could identify with how I was feeling. Maya is like my biggest supporter."

"Maya also found out how much I like to watch soccer. She spoke to my parents, and encouraged me to play soccer; that really helped me to make friends. They were resistant at first, but they slowly warmed to me playing soccer. Maya seems to have charmed my dad." Sema giggled, and Mrs. Abadi smiled. "She also talked to him about me going to university as well – if I can get a scholarship. If I were back in Syria, I would be thinking about marriage right now – but, instead, I am finishing high school, and I really want to go to a university.

Mrs. Saylor turned to Maya, "Maya - I've heard so many good things about you. – Can you tell me more about your experience this past year as a mentor for World Relief? What have you learned from this experience?"

"Well, for one thing, I have learned to slow down and to take my time. Our culture puts so much emphasis on multi-tasking and accomplishing many things at once; and when I visit with Sema and her family, there are social rituals (we have tea and talk before diving into work) – and, afterwards, I am often invited to stay for a meal. There is a genuine sense of caring and welcoming in her home that I have not been used to in any of the places I have lived. I had to change my approach, from always being in a hurry to get things done and move to the next thing – to just enjoy being in the moment. I can honestly say that this experience has made me more thoughtful and considerate of other worldviews.

I also expanded my professional network, thanks to you Cheryl, and World Relief. I appreciate the valuable connections that you were able to facilitate in learning how to mentor someone from another culture. Assistance with language barriers was helpful in working with Sema's family and making her more comfortable, although she already had a pretty good command of English. Many of these contacts will help me in the future, especially when I start my studies in immigration law.

"That's great, Maya. And how demanding will your new school schedule be? Do you think you can handle continuing the mentorship?"

"Yes! Sema and I have talked about it a little bit, but not formally. We would like to continue to meet throughout the summer once a week, and when the school year begins, we will continue to hang out on Google once a month. If she finds she needs more than that, can she call you for help in finding someone else?"

"Of course. Sema, don't hesitate to contact me if you find you need more assistance as the year progresses," Cheryl responded. She paused for a moment, and then turned back to Maya. "So, have you planned a celebration for the end of the school year and your one year of mentorship?

"Yes!" Maya answered. "We are going to our favorite sushi restaurant this weekend to celebrate! Sema's friends Serena and Ami are going to join us there. Also, I have a small gift for you Sema." She handed a brown paper-wrapped package with a bow to Sema. "It's fragile, so don't drop it!" Maya warned.

Sema ripped the wrapping off, her eyes watered, and she smiled. "Oh Maya, this is so lovely!"

She turned to show the framed picture to her mother. "Look, Mama! This is from the day Maya took me to the poppy fields!" It was a photo of Sema lying in the fields with her shoes sticking out.

Mrs. Abadi took the photo from Sema, and her eyes glistened. "Shukran, Maya. Thank you so much."

"You are so welcome Mrs. Abadi. Sema has really taught me so much, and I am so grateful for this opportunity to have mentored. I would be happy to help her find a college to apply for next year, and to start the application process."

Amidst the tears and hugging, Mrs. Saylor chimed in, "Well ladies, I have another Zoom (maybe meeting instead of another Zoomcll?)call to get to, but I am going to leave some paperwork with you to fill out, as well as a new mentorship agreement to fill out that spells out what you shared with me about the new meeting schedule, and what Sema hopes to accomplish. Maya, you have my number and, if things become overwhelming with your new school schedule, or Sema – if you feel you need more study time with a mentor, please reach out to me."

Good Afternoon Mrs. Cheryl Saylor, how are you doing?

"I am doing very well, how are you Daon?"

"I am doing well! The mentor match between Joe and Isaiah went extremely well. Isaiah leaves to go to Hampton University on Friday, but I don't want to get ahead of myself. Let's wait a few more minutes for Troy and Danise to join us."

Bing-Boom (The sound of an incoming Zoom caller)

"Good afternoon, guys! How is everyone?" Troy's countenance and energy always brightened the room, even if it was a Zoom call.

"No worries, Troy! We are just glad that you were able to join us! How are things in Nashville?" Cheryl asked.

Bing-Boom (The sound of an incoming zoom caller)

"Hey, team! Tell me something positive that happened in your life today!" Danise chimed in, as everyone on the call groaned.

"The most positive thing that is happening in my life today is the fact that I have an opportunity to connect with you guys! I promise that I won't hold you long. In fact, I have only scheduled this call to last thirty minutes. My purpose for this call is pretty simple. You guys are extremely familiar with the **Six Elements of Effective Practice for Mentoring.** I wanted to get your thoughts and feedback with regard to your mentor-mentee matches; specifically, I would like your suggestions and recommendations for best practices as you close out your matches. Danise, can you begin?"

"Sure Daon, this has been a great mentoring year at Strategion. Rena and Alexandra were a great match and as you know. We only require our mentors to engage in a one-year commitment. We believe that proper closure is critical in order to affirm the contributions of both the mentor and the mentee. We utilize three primary methods for effective closure at the end of the engagement:

1.   *the interview,*
2.   *the survey,*
3.   *the Strategion EMME (Exceptional Mentor Mentee Extravaganza) Awards.*

Troy was the first to chime in, "Wow! EMME Awards!"

Danise smiled, "We started the EMME Awards last year. We talk it up and really make it a big deal. It is a company-wide event, and we make sure that all of our executives attend. We have special presentations from our CEO, and typically invite a guest speaker to deliver our keynote. No one knows this yet, but Rena and Alexandra have received the most votes for our **Match of the Year Award**! And one thing that I really appreciate about Alexandra is her **LIONIZING** focus. Whenever, Alexandra has an opportunity, she does everything in her power to promote Rena's accomplishments and talents. This has really helped Rena's confidence. At first, she was shy, but even her co-workers have noticed the transformation. I firmly believe that Alexandra played a key role in her development."

Cheryl chimed in, "That is absolutely incredible! I love the way that your company incorporates celebration and recognition. It is so critically important to acknowledge the contributions and time commitment of our mentors. They are on the frontlines, and they can make or break a program. You guys know that Maya got accepted into Yale Law School, so the staff at WRO and I have been thinking of creative ways to keep their match going."

"Wow, congratulations, Cheryl. You are really doing an excellent job!" Troy knew the hard work that Cheryl had put in to find a successful multicultural match.

Cheryl smiled, "Thanks Troy, you are so kind. We had them both complete surveys, and I literally just left Sema's Mom's house where we assessed the mentoring relationship, and the steps moving forward from here. I am pretty sure that they are going to complete another mentorship agreement that outlines how they will keep their match alive. Maya really embraced the concept of **LAUNCHING Sema into success**. I am really excited."

Troy chimed in, "Well, let me give you guys a heads up. You guys well know that mentoring is hard. Mentors and mentees usually have many things on their respective tables between work, personal projects, and their training paths. Learning opportunities are infinite, but available time is not. Shawn and Anderson are finishing a lot stronger than they started, that's for sure! We had a Zoom check-in call earlier this week, and they seemed to be doing quite well. I also had them complete an assessment, but it was really good to see them both on the Zoom call. Their interaction has really moved from transaction to transformation, and it appears that Shawn is really growing in his new position and career. I agree with you, Cheryl that the mentee that is **LAUNCHED** by their mentor has a decided advantage moving forward."

"I really appreciated my team's hard work. I knew that they were all extremely busy, so I need to wrap it up. It is so good to hear that all of you are doing well. Thanks for keeping me in the loop with your best practices. Mentoring is never easy, and I really appreciate that we have formed this network to support one another, and to bounce ideas off each other. As you know, Isaiah is headed off to Hampton University next week. And Joe has been an absolutely champion mentor. Although their mentoring engagement has ended, Joe went over and above the call of duty connecting Isaiah with his network, and even setting up Isaiah's Linked-In profile. With everything that Joe has done, I am absolutely sure that Isaiah will hit the ground running next week."

"So, team, that's all I needed. I just wanted to get your thoughts, ideas, and best practices with regard to closure. From your comments, I would agree that assessment, launching, and lionizing are all powerful tools to utilize at the end of the mentor-mentee relationship. Without question, effective mentoring requires a lot of work. And, as you know, I always say that **mentoring is more than a mere definition or theoretical framework; it is an art!** Just like faint brushes on a blank canvas or soft notes melodiously whispered in the midst of a concerto, effective mentoring requires both theory and practice, structure and improvisation, and legato and staccato to produce the harmonious blend of personal and professional success in the life of a protégé (and of a mentor, too!). Yes! Mentoring is an Art!"

APPENDIX

The collaborative synergy that results from a mentor and mentee LABORING to achieve and accomplish goals yields multiple results and rewards. Here are four of them:

1. Mentor & Mentee Relationship Benefits

During the goal-setting process, the mentor-mentee relationship is strengthened and transformed as the mentor has an opportunity to see deeper into the personal and professional motivations of the mentee. What makes the mentee tick? What are his/her underlying motivations and ambitions? How does the mentee view his/her life purpose or career trajectory? All these questions are answered during the goal-setting process, thus allowing the mentor to peer into the heart of the mentee.

2. Mentor & Mentee Become Process Oriented

The goal-setting process is a profound lesson in process management. True, the goal-setting process forces the mentee to think about his/her desired destination carefully and systematically; however, the process also requires the mentee to identify the specific tasks that will be required to reach said destination. In other words, the goal-setting process forces the mentee to think about the journey (how he/she is going to complete their tasks), instead of just the end destination. Educating, encouraging, equipping, and empowering the mentee to create a detailed actionable plan will not only activate and solidify the mentee's resolve for attainment, but will also serve as the impetus for a powerful, collaborative relationship. This synergistic effect is a by-product of the process-oriented mindset inevitably produced as the mentee focuses on his/her journey.

3. Mentor & Mentee Understand the Importance of Accountability and Accountable Relationships

Another by-product of the goal-setting process is an understanding of what it means to be held accountable for one's tasks and responsibilities. During the regular mentor-mentee meetings, the mentor should make it a point to systematically run down the list of deliverables that had been established at the previous meeting. Kudos are provided when deliverables are produced, when assessments are discussed, and when roadblocks and obstacles prevent the mentee from completing an assignment. These moments of reflection can only take place in the context of an accountable relationship in which the hard questions are not afraid to be asked or addressed.

4. Mentee Develops a Sense of Self-Empowerment

No words can describe a mentee's feelings of pride and self-actualization when the goals that he/she had systematically calculated are subsequently achieved and celebrated. From a mentor's perspective, the value of these wins should never be minimized or underestimated. Celebrate every victory! Success is a powerful motivator, and the mentee can use successful moments to emphasize her/his ability to achieve positive results from the goal-setting process. These feelings of pride and self-actualization then become the driving force to envision greater goals and opportunities for personal and professional growth.

SPEAKING ENGAGEMENTS

Daon McLarin Johnson is an excellent speaker. He has mastered *The Art of Effective Mentoring*. Daon has spent over 20 years mentoring both young adults and adults to achieve the impossible by sharing tried and true techniques.

He offers keynote speeches to organizations, corporations, fraternities and sororities, colleges and schools. He offers in-house seminars that are customized to maximize attendees' experiences.

BULK PURCHASES

The Art of Effective Mentoring is available at special quantity discounts for bulk purchases. This book is perfect for employee gifts, sales promotions, premiums, or fund-raising.

To book Daon for your next conference or in-house event, please contact him at www.TheArtofEffectiveMentoring.com.

CPSIA information can be obtained
at www.ICGtesting.com
Printed in the USA
LVHW081132310821
696561LV00003B/31